GET THE FACTS YOU NEED.

DON'T MISS . . .

A crib vibrator to soothe fussy newborns. (But what about a womb-sound machine?)

The best buy in baby wipes. (Should you get that wipe warmer too?)

A wonderful fabric for baby bibs. (Now what's the optimal number of bibs to buy?)

The best travel toys. (Will the one for infants really keep them occupied?)

High-tech high chairs with terrific features. (Should you toss out the classic wooden ones?)

The essentials of the perfect potty. (But will toilet learning accelerate if you also purchase a potty video?)

A baby swing—a must-have for exhausted parents. (Should you also get a doorway jumper?)

Adorable table and chair sets. (Wood, plastic, or none at all?)

PARENTS PICKS
BABY GEAR

DON'T MISS THESE
OTHER Parents PICKS

THE PARENTS ANSWER BOOK

YOUR ONE-YEAR-OLD

YOUR TWO-YEAR-OLD

THE PARENTS PARTY BOOK

THE ACTIVITY BOOK

IT WORKED FOR ME!

AVAILABLE FROM
ST. MARTIN'S PAPERBACKS

Parents **Picks**

Baby Gear

Everything You Need to Clothe, Feed, Transport, Protect, Entertain, and Care for Your Baby from Birth to Age Three

By the Editors of *Parents* magazine with Debra Wise

Foreword by Sally Lee, Editor-in-Chief

Illustrated by Laura Hartman Maestro

St. Martin's Paperbacks

BABY GEAR

Copyright © 2001 by Roundtable Press, Inc., and G+J USA Publishing.

Cover photo © credit Sara Hutchins/Taxi

Library of Congress Catalog Card Number: 2001019353

ISBN: 0-312-98875-3
EAN: 80312-98875-3

Printed in the United States of America

Roundtable Press, Inc., edition published 2001
St. Martin's Paperbacks edition / September 2004

St. Martin's Paperbacks are published by St. Martin's Press, 175 Fifth Avenue, New York, NY 10010.

10 9 8 7 6 5 4 3 2 1

CONTENTS

Chapter 7
**Outdoor Safety
and Fun**

FOREWORD

Before I became a mother, I used to tease my sister-in-law, a mother of two, because she arrived for every family visit with enough baby gear to fill a small department store. Now as a mother of a three- and six-year-old, who currently owns four strollers, five potties, and who won't travel without a trunk full of brightly-colored plastic essentials, I have a little more empathy.

Although many of us are lucky enough to get advice (and hand-me-downs) from friends or family, parents' needs vary greatly depending on where you live, the size of your family, your budget, living space, and lifestyle. *Baby Gear* takes all of these factors into account and offers straightforward advice on which products you should *really* buy and which features to look for in everything from pacifiers to pajamas to play yards.

Baby Gear can definitely save you time and money. More importantly, it will help you to keep your child safe, healthy, comfortable, and happy.

Sally Lee
Editor-in-Chief

Chapter 1

The Nursery

Setting up your baby's nursery is one of the first labors of love you'll perform for your child. The primary thing on your mind, of course, will be creating a comfortable, soothing haven for your baby—and for you. Whatever your decorating style, you'll want to make sure that the furnishings and accessories you choose are practical and safe. Don't take it for granted that everything marketed for newborns is babyproof. Decorative items like quilts, pillows, and crib bumpers can present dangers such as too-long ties and loosely sewn-on buttons. Bookcases can tip; rocking chairs can pinch tiny fingers. A bit of research and some common sense is all it takes to ensure that you'll create a room that's not only adorable but safe and sound.

Beds and Bedding

Cribs
Age: Birth–3 years

Since your baby will spend more of her time asleep than awake during her first year, the crib is the most important item in the nursery. The place where your baby sleeps should be comfortable, cozy, and, most of all, safe. It's best to buy a new crib if possible so that it will meet the current standards set by the U.S. Consumer Product Safety Commission (CPSC) as certified by the Juvenile Products Manufacturers Association (JPMA). Surprisingly, cribs are associated with more children's deaths than any other juvenile product (walkers included). And most of these accidents were attributed to old cribs that failed to meet current safety standards.

The most common hazards of older cribs include slats that are too far apart (there should be no more than 2⅜ inches between slats), corner posts that extend beyond the top of the end panel, paint that contains lead (any paint made before 1980 may), and cutouts on the headboard or footboard that could entrap head, hands, or feet.

To ensure the safety of your crib, shop at a reputable retailer and look for the JPMA seal (usually on the footboard). Don't assume that a pricier crib is a safer crib; a basic $100 model may be every bit as good (and often as good-looking) as the fanciest designer brands.

After establishing the crib's safety, the next thing you should do is determine which features are necessary.

Mattress

Most cribs don't come with a mattress, so you will need to buy one separately. They come in one standard size, in either foam or coil (innerspring) models, and they should fit snugly against the crib's rail. Foam mattresses are lighter and less expensive, but they provide less support. Remember, your tiny newborn will probably still be sleeping on this mattress

Crib

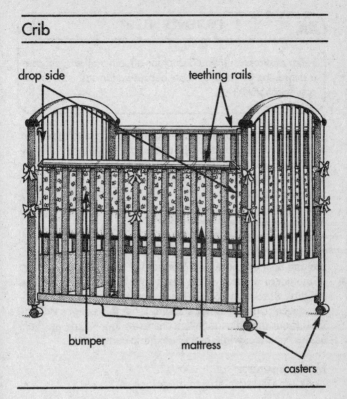

drop side

teething rails

bumper

mattress

casters

when she tops 30 pounds, so investing in a good coil mattress makes sense.

The quality of innerspring mattresses varies, and here price is often a good guideline to determine quality. More expensive mattresses usually have a higher coil count and therefore offer more support. Aim for 150 to 160 coils—a lower-count mattress will get lumpy, while a higher-count one will not really affect your baby's comfort.

Some products on the market claim to lower the risk of Sudden Infant Death Syndrome (SIDS), including a mattress

⚠ **PARENTS ALERT** ⚠

Foam mattresses: If you do opt for a foam mattress, choose a dense, top-of-the-line model because a too-soft mattress is a suffocation risk.

with a built-in fan and a sheet-and-mattress pad to maximize airflow. According to the CPSC, there is no evidence that using these products reduces the risk of SIDS, and babies cannot safely be placed on their stomachs to sleep using these or any other products.

Mattress height

Make sure your crib's mattress can be adjusted to at least two heights: high, so that you don't have to strain your back picking up a newborn, and low, so that a standing baby can't climb out of the crib. Many cribs have three or four mattress heights, which can be convenient for your baby's intermediate stages (sitting but not standing), but this is not essential. Check out the adjustment mechanism, too—some are very easy to operate, while others are quite complicated.

Mattress support

Look for a sturdy platform of springs.

Drop side

At least one side of the crib should have a mechanism that allows it to lower so you can pick up your baby without having to lean over the side. Many have a foot release that requires you to lift up the side while pushing a bar with your foot. Others have hand latches. Choose one that is easy for you to operate and locks back into position easily. Double-drop sides are not usually necessary, since most cribs are positioned against a wall. You may actually find that you rarely drop even one side, since it can be easy to lift a small baby or a standing toddler without lowering the side.

Stability
Shake the crib to see if it wobbles—many do. Cribs on wheels tend to be shakier. The more stable the crib, the more comfortable it will be for your baby.

Ease of assembly
Look at the directions even if you plan to have your crib delivered and set up. You will want to dismantle it one day, and perhaps set it up again for another child.

Casters
Metal or thick plastic casters are superior to thin plastic wheels, which don't roll easily and can crack.

Teething rail
Many cribs have a strip of plastic along the top of the rails for babies to teethe on. This is not essential since you can buy a separate teething rail if need be.

Drawer
Some high-end cribs come with a useful, built-in storage drawer.

Bedding
Age: Birth–3 years

Mattress pad
Use a quilted mattress pad (much like the one on your own bed) for your baby's crib. Those that wrap completely around the mattress won't bunch up and therefore make for a smoother sleeping surface. But flat ones make crib changes easier. Some pads have a plastic lining to protect the mattress, but this is unnecessary since crib mattresses themselves are vinyl-covered. You'll only need one or two mattress pads if you also use a waterproof pad on top of the mattress pad.

> ⚠️ **PARENTS ALERT** ⚠️
>
> **Fitted sheets:** Always use a fitted crib sheet over a quilted mattress pad to ensure that the sheet does not come untucked and expose the vinyl mattress covering, which would be a suffocation risk. Never put a baby on any crib mattress unless it is first covered by a fitted sheet.

Waterproof pad

Waterproof pads are thin sheets of rubber coated with cotton flannel on both sides. They come in both crib and bassinet sizes and cover the entire top of the mattress. The waterproof pad is placed between the quilted mattress pad and the fitted sheet to protect the mattress and mattress pad. Waterproof pads are easy to change because they lie on top of the mattress. Buy two to four, depending on how often you do laundry.

Sheet

For safety's sake, use only fitted crib, cradle, and bassinet sheets and use them only on the mattress size they are intended for. Some fitted crib sheets even come with ties at the corners to secure them to the crib rails.

Sheets come in percale (woven cotton or polyester/cotton blends), flannel, and jersey knit—and in myriad colors and prints. Although percale offers the greatest color and pattern selection, flannel and knit sheets are usually softer. Percale blends can be scratchy and tend to pill with repeated washing. Sheets with a high thread count (at least 200) feel softest and wear best. Three or four crib sheets should be enough unless your child wets excessively or spits up a lot.

Sheet protector

Changing the linens on a crib is not an easy task—it usually involves removing the bumpers and taking out the whole

⚠ **PARENTS ALERT** ⚠

Top sheets and pillows: Never use a top sheet or pillow in a crib. Both pose a suffocation risk and are unnecessary for the baby's comfort.

mattress. A sheet protector puts an extra, easy-to-change layer between your baby's moistest spots and the sheet.

One type of sheet protector, often known as a "crib bib," is meant to be placed under the baby's head. They are typically made of a double layer of terry cloth and quilted cotton about a foot wide and the length of the crib. They tie or Velcro to the crib slats and can be changed quickly if the baby spits up. These should be pulled tightly across the mattress and tied securely to prevent the baby from getting caught underneath. When the baby starts moving around, crib bibs should no longer be used.

Also available are crib sheet protectors that cover the entire top of the sheet. These are typically a layer of absorbent material sandwiched between a soft fabric top and a waterproof bottom. They also secure with ties or snaps. Although convenient, whole-sheet protectors must be very carefully secured to prevent any part of the baby from getting caught between the sheet protector and the sheet.

Bumpers

A crib bumper lines the four inner sides of the crib and protects the baby from bumping her head or body on the rails. Typically, the bumper also makes the main fashion statement in the crib and ranges in design from simple solid-color cotton to more decorative varieties with oversize quilted headboards in designer fabrics. The basic model is every bit as serviceable as the deluxe, as long as it meets certain safety standards. The ties that attach the bumpers to the crib rails should be sewn securely to the pads, and there

⚠️   **PARENTS ALERT**   ⚠️

Bedding ornamentation: There should be no ornamentation on bumpers or any other bedding that could pose a choking or strangulation hazard. This includes buttons, ribbons, flimsy ruffles, or any other decorations that a baby could pull off and put in her mouth.

should be ties on both the top and the bottom edges of the bumper. Trim off any excess length after tying to prevent the baby from becoming entangled in the ties. The filling should be thick and firm. Synthetic batting often stands up to the wash better than pure cotton.

The CPSC recommends that parents remove bumpers from the crib as soon as the baby is able to pull herself up so that she can't use them to climb out of the crib. We disagree for three reasons. First, it makes more sense to have bumpers in place for a bigger, more mobile child who moves around in her sleep than for a tiny newborn who remains static in the middle of the crib. Second, bumpers make poor footholds, since they tend to squash down when stepped upon. Third, if a child can climb out of a crib using bumpers, chances are good that she can escape just as handily without them (time to start thinking about a bed!). If you do decide to leave the bumpers in place, check the ties often to make sure they remain secure.

Blanket

Although it's fine to let an appropriately dressed baby sleep with no covers when it's warm, you'll need a blanket if nights turn chilly. Many crib bedding sets include a thick quilt, which is too heavy for a newborn. For babies younger than one year, look for a soft crib-sized or smaller receiving blanket that will be warm without being heavy or bulky. Good fabrics for this age are cotton in a jersey or thermal knit, chenille, flannel, fleece (very warm), and brushed acrylic. Make sure the blanket has well-bound edges that

⚠ **PARENTS ALERT** ⚠

Quilts: Never cover a newborn with a heavy quilt or comforter, because a small baby can become trapped beneath it. This is both uncomfortable and a suffocation risk. Never use down or wool.

won't fray and that it doesn't have fringe. Avoid wool, which can be scratchy, and down, which is too puffy. Both can also cause allergic reactions.

Older babies—who can roll over both ways and have full head and neck control—can handle a heavier blanket, but a big, puffy quilt is still better used as a wall hanging. Most babies and small children don't like heavy covers, anyway. Once your baby is older than six months, a thin cotton quilt is fine. Look for a pliable, tightly stitched quilt with only a small amount of batting inside. Any quilt with enough batting to spring back when you pinch it is too thick. As with bumpers, make sure that blankets and quilts are free of anything that could choke or strangle: buttons, ribbons, fringe, loose appliqués, knots of thread or yarn (often found on handmade quilts), or loose stitching. If in doubt, use it for decoration and cover the baby with something safe and simple.

Dust ruffle
A crib dust ruffle is for decoration only.

Bassinets
Age: Birth–4 months
Although it's fine for a baby to sleep in a crib from the time she comes home from the hospital, a bassinet provides a cozy, comforting, and portable place for a newborn to sleep. Many new parents keep a bassinet beside their bed for those first few months of middle-of-the-night feedings. And in a two-story house, a downstairs bassinet saves you from having to walk upstairs every time the baby falls asleep.

HOW TO MAKE UP A CRIB

Many prospective parents have no idea how much work goes into making up a crib. Because the mattress fits so snugly against the crib rails, it's best to start by removing the mattress from the crib and placing it on the floor. If you're using a dust ruffle, place it over the mattress support (springs) and arrange it evenly around the sides.

Cover the mattress with a crib-sized quilted mattress pad. Then place a flat waterproof crib pad on top of the mattress pad. Finally, cover the waterproof pad with a fitted crib sheet.

Return the mattress to the crib. Place the bumper pad in the crib and securely fasten the ties to the rails. Double-check that all the ties are firmly fastened and trim any excess tie. If you like, add a sheet protector, also making sure the ties are secured. A lightweight blanket completes your baby's bed.

Bassinets are typically oval and basketlike in shape, and they come in several different styles. The most traditional is made of woven wicker and stands on wheeled legs. It is usually lined with quilted fabric or vinyl and has a thin foam mattress, also vinyl covered. Some wicker bassinets have a hood to protect the baby from the sun. Bassinets of this type are usually quite reasonable in price and can be found at both discount and specialty stores. The mattress is included, but you will need specially sized bassinet sheets and mattress protectors. You can also get a fancy bassinet skirt that looks like a big dust ruffle and covers the outside of the bassinet and its legs. Some models convert to co-sleepers or come with convenient storage shelves underneath.

Another type of bassinet is the Moses basket, which is woven of flexible rush and has handles and no legs. While adorable and very portable, Moses baskets are not very practical. They tend to be very small and are not usually suitable for a baby older than about six weeks. For safety reasons, they must sit on the floor, and bending down to pick up a baby can be very hard on your back. It's also unsafe to carry the basket around with the baby inside. If you receive a Moses basket as a gift, you may want to use it as an auxiliary bassinet and portable bed.

Newer bassinets have elements of both the traditional standing model and the Moses basket. The basket part consists of a metal frame covered with white or printed fabric (which can be removed for washing), and sits on top of a folding metal frame complete with casters, and often a wire or mesh basket below. Some models perform double duty: the casters retract into the frame and allow the base to rock like a cradle. This bassinet offers the best of both worlds, as it may be placed on the frame or lifted off and carried by handles similar to those of a Moses basket. As with the Moses basket, you should not carry it with the baby inside. With or without the frame, this type of bassinet moves easily from room to room and floor to floor, and is also an excellent first travel bed. More expensive than a wicker bassinet, but still reasonably priced, this is an item that is well worth buying for your first baby and handing down to future family members.

Cradles
Age: Birth–6 months
Like a bassinet, a cradle is a small, cozy place for a baby to sleep during her first few months. Unlike a bassinet, a cradle is not portable. On the positive side, you can't beat a cradle's rocking motion for soothing a baby to sleep. There are two types of cradle: the one that sits on rockers on the floor, and the one that is suspended between two posts. Whichever model you choose, look for a stable base and a smooth, quiet rocking motion. When your baby starts moving around and trying to roll over, it's time to retire the cradle.

Be wary of old cradles. As with antique cribs, old cradles

may be covered with lead paint or have slats that are too far apart to be safe. They also tend to be rickety and may not be able to support your baby's weight.

If you decide to use a cradle, you'll need all the bedding items you would for a crib, but in cradle size. Look for a thick, firm foam mattress, bumpers with ties, tight-fitting sheets and pads, and a lightweight blanket.

Co-sleepers
Age: Birth–6 months
Co-sleepers enable parents and infants to sleep together for the first few months. The co-sleeper is the size of a portable crib and attaches to the side of the parents' bed. One side of the co-sleeper can be folded down to eliminate any barrier between you and the baby. Your baby is within arm's reach when she wakes up to nurse.

Most co-sleepers consist of a padded nylon and mesh covering and a collapsible metal frame. They convert into a play yard, a portable crib, and a portable changing table, and fold into a carrying case for storage. Some higher-priced wooden units convert into a bassinet, a desk, or an easel when your co-sleeping days are over.

A bassinet placed next to the bed serves a similar purpose to a co-sleeper, but parents may feel closer without the extra "wall" between them and their baby. The co-sleeper that converts into a play yard (the mesh type) is a good value, because it costs less than it would to buy a portable crib and a bassinet. The drawbacks are that co-sleepers cannot be moved from room to room unless they are folded down, and they tend to be a bit smaller than regular portable play yards.

Toddler Beds
Age: 18 months–4 years
A toddler bed is a miniature bed that uses the crib mattress and sits very low to the ground. It's meant as a transitional step between a crib and a twin bed. Toddler beds can range from inexpensive metal or plastic models to quite pricey furniture-quality wooden ones. Some cribs convert into tod-

dler beds. There are also whimsical toddler beds shaped like race cars, boats, cottages, and the like.

A toddler bed is not a necessity—a child can move right from a crib to a twin bed with a guard rail. In several situations, however, it makes sense to use one: If you have a very active baby who climbs out of her crib before she's two, switching to a toddler bed (or a mattress on the floor) will help prevent injuries. A toddler bed is also practical if your child's room is very small (or is shared with an older sibling).

But if you're moving your child out of her crib to free it for a new baby, a toddler bed is not such a good idea, because you would need to buy a second crib mattress. If your first child will be younger than two when her sibling is born, consider keeping the new baby in a bassinet for the first few months. If the older child will be under 18 months when the new baby arrives, you'll probably want to buy a second crib.

Toddler bedding
Since toddler beds use crib mattresses, there's no need to buy new linens for them. There are, however, lines of bedding specifically made for toddler beds. These often include top sheets and comforters that are fitted at one end so they stay tucked in at the foot of the bed, as well as a mini pillow case. If you want to use a pillow—which is still not necessary but is no longer dangerous after age two—look for one that's made for toddlers. Toddler pillows are small, relatively flat, and covered in soft flannel or cotton knit.

Bed Rails
Age: 18 months and up
Bed rails make the transition to a big bed safer and less scary for your child by reducing the risk of falling out. The rail's anchors fit between the mattress and the box spring to hold the rail in place. Most rails are hinged and swing down and out of the way so the child can get in and out or a parent can sit on the edge of the bed. Bed rails come in wooden, plastic, metal, and metal-framed nylon mesh styles. Look for one

---

⚠️   **PARENTS ALERT**   ⚠️

Falling out of bed: Don't assume that a bed rail will always prevent your child from falling out of bed. Active sleepers may move down to the end of the bed and fall out. Cushion hard floors with pillows or a folded comforter. Or consider placing the mattress on the floor until the child outgrows falling.

---

with a mechanism that stays locked in the upright position even with a heavy child leaning against it, but that also operates easily when you want to fold it down.

Absorbent Bed Pads
Age: 2 years and up

Whether your child is toilet-taught or not when she moves into a big bed, remember that the mattress she will be sleeping on will not be vinyl covered. One or two super-absorbent pads made for twin (or full) beds are a good investment. These three-layer pads are cotton on the top and vinyl on the bottom, and have an absorbent middle layer that wicks moisture away from the child's skin (similar to a disposable diaper). The pads may be placed under or on top of the fitted sheet. They are a great alternative to crinkly, uncomfortable plastic sheets.

Furniture

Changing Tables
Age: Birth–3 years

You'll be changing a lot of diapers over the first two to three years of your baby's life, so it makes sense to have a convenient place to do it. Although any flat surface that's the right height (a dresser, table, or counter) can be pressed into use as a diaper changing station, changing tables tend to be safer

TWO'S COMPANY—PLANNING A NURSERY FOR MULTIPLES

Planning a nursery for two or more may seem challenging, but it's actually not much different from planning for one. The big difference, of course, is that you'll need space for both (or all) of your babies to sleep. If the room is big enough, a full-sized crib for each baby is the best option. This will provide the most comfort and privacy for each child as she grows. It's worth moving dressers, storage shelves, even a changing station elsewhere to free up space for separate cribs.

If space is tight, you may want to set up one crib with a divider for twins. Similar to a miniature bumper, this foam-covered pad is placed horizontally across the middle of the crib to divide it in half. One baby sleeps on each side, horizontally or vertically, depending on her size. This is a good solution if you plan on moving one of the babies into another room or moving to larger quarters when the twins are too big to share a crib. (Newborn babies can sleep in any space that is big enough to hold them; they don't need extra room around them. Just make sure the bumpers aren't so close that the baby's face is pressed against them.) Some parents also place twins together in an undivided crib—either touching or at opposite ends—and find that it soothes the babies to sleep together. Try it to see what works best for your babies.

Another option for close quarters is two bassinets or portable cribs/play yards (see pages 114–115). This, of course, is a temporary solution that works only for the first few months.

Other than two cribs—and twice as many diapers—multiples can get by perfectly well with the same nursery furnishings as a singleton. One dresser, one changing table, and one generously proportioned rocking chair are all you need. Try to optimize your storage space in

---

TWO'S COMPANY—PLANNING A
NURSERY FOR MULTIPLES
(continued)

---

any way you can, whether that means choosing a changing table that doubles as a dresser, outfitting the closet with drawers and shelves, or hanging shelves to utilize wall space.

Many new parents of multiples worry that their babies will constantly wake each other up if they share a room. In most cases this is not true, especially for the first couple of years. Babies that have been in the womb together tend to take each other's presence for granted, and many are even comforted by having their siblings close by. When you think about how special the bond between your multiples will grow to be, it makes sharing close quarters seem like a privilege rather than a penalty.

---

for the child and more comfortable for the caregiver. It also allows you to store diapers, wipes, ointments, first-aid supplies, and even linens in one easily accessible place.

There are two basic types of changing tables: the freestanding changing table with open shelves and the dresser/changing table combination, with or without a flip top.

The freestanding changing table usually consists of three wide shelves. The top shelf is the changing surface and is covered with a removable vinyl-covered foam pad (which itself is covered with a removable terry-cloth or quilted fabric case). There are open shelves or drawers underneath. Most changing tables have a rail or rim around the changing area to discourage the baby from rolling off. It is safest to have a rim of two to three inches all the way around. Most also have attached safety straps.

If space is tight, or if you don't like the idea of buying a piece of furniture that will become obsolete when your baby is

WHAT TO KEEP ON THE CHANGING TABLE

Organize your changing table so that the things you use most often are within easy reach. If you have an open-shelf model, use baskets to help keep small items together. Here's what you'll need:

- Disposable diapers, or cloth diapers and diaper covers
- Baby wipes (alcohol-free and unscented for newborns)
- Diapering creams or ointments (for preventing and treating rashes)
- Baby moisturizer (unscented)
- Mineral oil or baby oil (for treating cradle cap)
- Rubbing alcohol (for umbilical cord stump care)
- Antibacterial ointment and gauze pads (for post-circumcision care)
- Cotton swabs
- Cotton balls
- Baby comb and brush
- First-aid supplies (until baby is old enough to be able to get into them; then lock them away)
- Cloth diapers (to use as shoulder protectors)
- Pacifiers
- Small toys (to distract the baby during changes)

out of diapers, opt for a dresser with a changing table top. Most of these feature flip tops that open up to create a larger changing area. Flip tops also have a folding changing pad. Although it's not as convenient to have to open a drawer to access diapering supplies, there are many plastic organizers on the market that can be hooked to the side of the changing surface or set nearby to keep supplies close at hand. Another feature to look for is a hutch or shelving unit behind the flip top for storage space. These units are very practical because they convert to bookshelves when your baby's changing table days are over.

Another very economical alternative is a changing sur-

⚠️   **PARENTS ALERT**   ⚠️

Changing-table safety: Never, ever leave a baby—or child of any age—unattended on a changing table for even a moment. Don't depend on a low rim or rail or the sides of a contoured pad to contain your baby—they are not meant for that purpose, only to discourage rolling. Even the youngest baby could propel herself off and experience a dangerous fall. Most changing tables and pads come with safety straps, which are admittedly inconvenient to use. But unless you have your hand on the baby at all times, use them.

face that attaches directly onto the crib rails. This device slides back and forth over the crib, and it positions your baby so that her feet are facing you (rather than her side); many parents actually find it easier to change a baby in this position. When not in use, the changing surface folds down to hang on the outside of the crib. Or, if you prefer, you can remove it completely between changes and store it elsewhere in the room.

Contoured changing pad

If you decide to press a regular dresser into service as a changing table (make sure it's a comfortable height), you'll need a contoured changing pad to place on top of it. This thick, vinyl-covered foam pad is scooped out in the middle to discourage the baby from rolling during a change, and includes a safety strap. It can also be used on most standard changing tables. For travel, look for a contoured pad that folds in half. These are thick and not appropriate for a diaper bag, however. Covers are available, too.

Dressers, Armoires, and Bookcases
Age: Birth and up

While the furniture you put in your baby's room certainly doesn't have to be made specifically for babies, it is wise to choose it with an eye toward safety and practicality. Look for sturdy pieces that are untippable (if you have any doubt at all about a piece's stability, attach it to the wall with bolts or special safety straps; *see pages 137–44 for babyproofing products*). Make sure the finish is smooth and, if the piece is old, that it is free of lead paint. Dresser drawers should glide easily. Drawer pulls must be attached securely, and be too large to swallow and too small to provide footholds for climbing.

Toy Chests
Age: Birth and up

Toy chests are a popular gift and a useful addition to the nursery, but they can pose safety hazards. If it is wooden, make sure the finish is smooth and free of splinters, and that there is no lead paint. The most important feature of a toy chest is its lid support, which should hold the top completely open, with no danger of its slamming down. A lightweight removable lid is another option. Also make sure that the lid or sides of the toy chest has air holes or some other type of ventilation in the event a child does get trapped inside. Open shelves or bins are the safest option of all.

Rocking Chairs and Gliders
Age: Birth and up

If there's room in the nursery, it's nice to have a rocking chair or glider to relax in, nurse, and lull your baby to sleep. Be sure to try it out before buying, because seats come in a variety of shapes and sizes. If you decide to get a glider—a chair that rests on a stationary base and glides back and forth on special tracks—look for one with a smooth and silent motion. While many parents find gliders extremely comfortable and enjoy using them for this reason, a traditional rocking chair soothes a baby just as effectively and has two advantages: it is more reasonably priced, and it can be used elsewhere in your home after you no longer need it in the nursery.

Other Accoutrements

Baby Monitors
Age: Birth and up

A baby monitor is a necessity if your baby will be sleeping out of earshot. The type you choose depends on the layout of your living space as well as the level of surveillance you desire. Remember that baby monitors operate on the same channels as cordless phones—and also your neighbors' monitors and phones—so it's not only your baby's nursery that is being bugged. If you have any concern about your signal being picked up, keep the monitor turned off when it is not in use.

Audio monitor

Most baby monitors are one-way intercom systems that consist of a transmitter, which is plugged into an outlet in the baby's room (or wherever she is sleeping), and a portable receiver, which can be plugged in or powered by batteries. Look for a monitor with as clear reception as possible. Interference tends to be greatest in heavily populated areas and when there's a portable phone in use nearby. If you live in an apartment building or in an urban area, you may find that a 900 MHz monitor gives you the least static and interference; the simplest models work just fine in suburban and rural areas.

Here are other features to look for:
- *Light display.* Lets you "see" the baby's sound level with signals that light up.
- *Extra receiver.* Super-convenient if you live in a two-story house.
- *Ultrasensitive reception.* Lets you hear every breath your baby takes and every move she makes.
- *Long-range reception.* Important if you plan to take the monitor outside while your baby sleeps.
- *Compact size.* Nice if you plan to carry the receiver

⚠️ **PARENTS ALERT** ⚠️

Tummy sleeping: Never put your baby to sleep on her stomach (unless your pediatrician has specifically instructed you to do so for a special reason). Recent studies have shown that placing babies on their backs or sides to sleep has reduced the rate of SIDS by up to 50 percent. An infant should be placed to sleep on her back until she can roll over and position herself independently (usually at four to five months). By this time, she will be so used to sleeping on her back that she will probably choose that position on her own.

around with you; not much of an issue if you plan to leave it in one place.

- *Rechargeable receiver.* Good money-saving feature if you plan to carry the monitor around or use it outdoors. For stationary indoor use, plug it in to get the best reception.
- *Warning light or alarm.* Signals when you are out of range.
- *Low-battery indicator.*
- *Two-way intercom.* Great for a large house, these work like walkie-talkies—you can press a button on either unit to speak to the person holding the other one, or even talk to your baby from another room. The only drawback: intercom monitors tend to be larger and heavier.

Video monitor

This monitor allows you to both hear and see your baby. In fact, the camera that transmits the image also has infrared capability that lets you see your child in the dark. The transmitter/camera can be placed on a table or dresser out of the baby's reach or mounted on the nursery wall. The receiver is a small black-and-white-TV monitor, which can be quite heavy and is not meant to be moved around a lot. Users give mixed reviews on the clarity of the visual reception. Again, the signal will probably not be as clear in densely populated areas. Video monitors cost several times as much as audio-only monitors, but you can use the receiver as a miniature black-and-white TV when your baby monitoring days are over.

Motion sensor

The newest development in baby monitor technology is the motion sensor, which monitors movement as well as sound. This is achieved by placing a sensor pad under the baby's mattress, which senses movement (including breathing) and sounds an alarm if the baby stops moving for a certain amount of time (20 seconds is common). This may be very reassuring to some parents, but it also has the potential to create anxiety through false alarms. If your baby is premature or at high risk for apnea or SIDS, consult with your doctor before depending on this type of monitor, as you may need a more sensitive machine.

Infant Positioners
Age: Birth–4 months

Often referred to as side sleepers or back sleepers, infant positioners are used to keep newborns in a safe sleeping position. The American Academy of Pediatrics now recommends back sleeping for all healthy, full-term babies to reduce the risk of SIDS. Although a newborn baby cannot roll from her back to her front, a sleep positioner provides a cozy place for a baby to sleep, with foam bolsters that fit around her body. If your doctor recommends side sleeping, you'll definitely need a positioner, since even newborns can roll from side to back or front. A side sleeper consists of two foam bolsters, wedge-shaped, attached to a piece of fabric. The baby is placed on her side between the bolsters, which keep her propped in position. This type of positioner may also be used for back sleeping. Remove the baby from the positioner when she begins trying to roll over—usually at around three or four months.

Organization Aids

There are many products designed to help organize the nursery, from special cotton swab dispensers to stuffed animal hammocks. Here is a partial list of the most popular ones. Check your local store or favorite Web site for more.

Diaper caddy

This clear plastic case hooks over the edge of the crib or changing table and keeps a supply of diapers close at hand. It can be helpful if your changing table does not have open shelves and you don't want to reach into a drawer to retrieve a diaper.

Diaper stacker

This is a long fabric bag with a hanger or hook at the top in which to stack diapers. The fabric often coordinates with the bedding pattern.

Rolling cart

This unit can be made of plastic or plastic-coated wire. It features drawers or bins topped with a surface about the height of a changing table and allows you to move supplies around the room. Rolling carts provide extra storage space that is especially nice to have if siblings are sharing a room.

Bin shelf

This low, bookshelf-sized rack comes with open plastic bins in which to organize toys or supplies. Be sure that anything stored in the bins is safe for the baby to handle.

Peg racks

Plain or decorative racks provide a place to hang jackets, hats, robes, or towels.

Hanging shelf organizer
This unit consists of several adjustable shelves inside a plastic casing that hangs from the closet rod. It's useful if you need more shelf space and have room in the closet.

Closet extender
This is a rod that hangs from the existing closet rod, providing a low hanging space that a child can reach.

Storage hammock
Elastic-bordered nylon netting becomes a great catch-all when hung in a corner, from the ceiling, or flat against a wall. It is especially great for corralling stuffed animals.

Toy chain
This is a plastic link chain with clips attached. It hangs from the ceiling and can be used to organize stuffed animals, puppets, hats, or mittens.

Miscellaneous Nursery Supplies
Here are a few more items you may want to include in your nursery.

Night-light
Look for a sturdy, unbreakable plastic light unless you plan on keeping it out of your child's reach. Battery-operated models are great because there are no cords to tug. Automatic shutoff is another nice feature. Be sure to place the night-light so it cannot shine directly into your baby's eyes.

Crib vibrator
Fussy newborns are often soothed by vibrations. This little battery-powered device attaches to the crib rail and creates vibrations similar to those of a moving car.

Crib cassette player
This is another device that attaches to the crib rail. Many crib cassette players include a night-light and a timer that turns off

the music and light after a certain time to conserve batteries. If you don't need the timer, keeping a regular portable cassette or CD player in the nursery is a more versatile option.

White-noise machine
Many parents swear by a white-noise machine for soothing their babies to sleep. This may be especially helpful if you live in a city or on a busy street.

Womb-sound machine
Often encased in the belly of a teddy bear, this little machine replicates intrauterine sounds, which may calm newborns. Look for a model that turns on when the baby cries, off when she's quiet.

Chapter 2

Baby Clothes

Planning a wardrobe for your baby can be both exciting and daunting. First-time parents often feel as if they have no idea what a baby really needs, so they tend to err on the side of excess, buying every item on a store's layette checklist to ensure that their baby doesn't lack anything essential. This chapter is meant to give you a working knowledge of what's actually necessary and what's nice to have, and how to get both at the best prices. As you shop, keep in mind that babies grow out of their clothes in a few months (sometimes weeks) and that it's likely that most of the gifts you receive will be clothes.

Just as with any baby gear, safety is always of primary concern with baby clothes. The pros and cons of flame-retardant sleepwear are discussed in this chapter, as well as the measures you should take to make sure that all the clothes you buy for your baby are safe and comfortable.

Diapers

Age: Birth–3 years

Since your baby will go through thousands of diapers, it makes sense to consider carefully what you use to cover his bottom. There are two basic choices: cloth or disposable. Each has benefits and drawbacks in the areas of comfort, convenience, and environmental impact. Here's how they stack up.

Disposable Diapers
Benefits and drawbacks

For sheer convenience, you can't beat disposables. There are no dirty diapers to tote, rinse, wash, or otherwise deal with. Disposables are easy to transport and put on because there are no separate fasteners, and they are faster and easier to take off too. Disposables also have the advantages of keeping the baby's skin drier and more comfortable (they wick away moisture into their absorbent cores), and leaking less because of their absorbent filling and custom-fit sizes. Disposables are also slim and trim under a baby's clothes.

The biggest drawback of disposables is that they're not ecologically friendly. It is estimated that each disposable diaper and the plastic bag it is thrown away in will take more than five hundred years to decompose in a landfill. What you might not have heard, though, is that landfill studies have consistently found that disposable diapers constitute no more than 1.4 percent by volume of the solid waste in the United States. Disposable diapers can also be expensive, but buying generic brands, buying in bulk, and using coupons can go a long way toward cutting costs. Ordering diapers over the Internet may also be less expensive than buying them at the grocery store— and they'll be delivered right to your doorstep.

All-natural disposables

Another alternative is all-natural disposable diapers, which are made of paper and filled with cotton and wood pulp. These diapers are definitely better for the planet, but they can be quite pricey (up to twice as expensive as regular disposables) and tend to leak. Although impractical for an infant, all-naturals may be a good choice for an older baby who wets less often.

Using disposables

If you decide to use disposable diapers, stock up when you're in your eighth month of pregnancy. Since newborn babies typically go through 10 to 12 diapers each day, it's a good idea to buy several packs. We recommend buying Size 1 diapers rather than newborn size. Size 1 is what most hospitals use and will fit most babies over six pounds. Newborn-size diapers—although they do have a convenient cutout for the umbilical cord stump—are more expensive, are outgrown quickly, and are too small for babies over eight pounds. You can always fill in with newborn diapers if your baby is premature or small.

Choosing a brand of disposables is a personal preference. You might want to buy two or three different ones in the beginning to compare.

Look for these features:
- *Outer covering.* May be thin plastic or clothlike paper backed in plastic. The clothlike covers are supposed to allow more air to circulate to the baby's skin, but they tend to get a bit damp on the outside when they get very wet.
- *Fasteners.* May be tape, Velcro tabs, or a combination of the two. Tape adheres better, but may be difficult to adjust or refasten.
- *Lotions.* Some diapers are treated with an emollient lotion meant to protect the baby's skin from diaper rash. Use of a barrier cream and frequent changing works just as well. If your baby has very sensitive skin and develops a rash that can be traced to the diaper, try a different brand.
- *Leg gathers.* Look for a diaper with several rows of elastic at the legs to prevent leakage.

Cloth Diapers
Benefits and drawback:

Some parents prefer cloth diapers because they like the idea of having natural cotton next to their baby's skin, and others because they believe them to be more ecologically sound. There is no doubt that using cloth saves precious landfill space. Cloth may also seem less wasteful because the diapers are reused rather than disposed of after each wearing. Finally, cloth diapers covered by cotton or wool diaper wraps let the baby's skin "breathe" and may reduce the incidence of diaper rash. This is only true, however, if the diapers are sterilized (by a diaper service or by boiling them at home) and are changed often—much more often than is necessary with disposables.

The biggest disadvantage to cloth diapers—and the one that causes many parents who start out committed to cloth to switch to disposables after a few weeks or months—is the extra work they create. Cloth diapers leak more, must be changed more often, and must be covered with plastic pants or a diaper cover *(see pages 31–32)*. Even if you use a diaper service, dirty diapers must be stored in a pail of disinfectant until pickup day—and no diaper pail will be completely odor-free. If a diaper service is not used, the pile of laundry (not only diapers and diaper covers, but also clothes and bedding) may seem insurmountable. Cloth diapers are also inconvenient for outings, since dirty diapers will need to be stored and brought home. They also take up more space in the diaper bag and require separate fasteners and covers.

On the environmental front, while it's true that cloth diapers don't clog landfills, they do require water and energy to clean. And the detergent and bleach used to sanitize cloth diapers pollute the water supply.

Finally, although cloth diapers may seem more economical, using a diaper service brings the cost to about the same as buying disposables. Although you can launder your own diapers, this is not recommended, since it is very difficult to sanitize diapers properly in a noncommercial washing machine.

Cloth-Diapering Steps

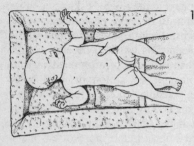

1. Fold the diaper square in half to form a rectangle. Then, take one short end of the rectangle and fold it toward you, about a third of the way down the diaper. Place your baby girl on top of the folded diaper, with her bottom centered on the double layers and her waist aligned with the top. For a boy, position the doubled-over fabric in front to provide extra padding for his penis. Place him on top of the diaper, aligning his waist with the top.

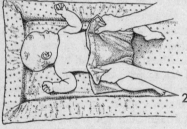

2. Pull the fabric up between your baby's legs and smooth it over her stomach.

3. Fasten the sides of the diaper with pins, one at a time. Be sure to keep your hand between the diaper and your baby's skin while pinning.

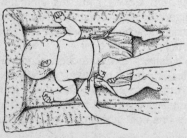

   If you like, cover the cloth diaper with a diaper cover.

Diaper services

If you decide to use cloth diapers, hire a diaper service well before your due date.

Here are some questions to ask a prospective service:

- How much does the service cost, and what is included in that cost? How many diapers will I receive each week? (Diaper services should deliver at least six dozen diapers a week.)
- Is there a special deal for multiples?
- Is the service personalized—i.e., will I get the same diapers back each week or receive different diapers?
- What will I need to do with the dirty diapers? Will the service provide a pail, liners, and disinfectant solution?
- Do the diapers come in different sizes? Does the service provide training pants?
- Are the diapers square or shaped? (This is a matter of personal preference. Shaped diapers do not require folding and fit into diaper covers better. Square diapers can be folded however you like.)
- Does the service provide diaper covers? Do they sell them or "rent" them? What styles and sizes are available?
- How often is pickup and on what day? Do I need to be home to receive my diapers?
- How are the diapers sterilized? What detergents are used? What happens if my baby's skin is sensitive to the fragrances or chemicals used?

It's a good idea to compare diapers and covers from several different services before making your decision.

Diaper covers

Happily, stiff, crinkly plastic pants are a thing of the past. Today's diaper covers are high-tech designs engineered to reduce leaks while keeping your baby's skin healthy. Diaper covers can be made of cotton or washable wool, with or without a polyurethane lining. Unlined covers are the most natural and breathable, but the lined ones do keep clothes and bedding drier. Like disposable diapers, diaper covers are sized according to the baby's weight and fastened with Velcro (some use snaps, but these provide less of a custom fit). Diapering a baby with a cloth diaper and diaper cover takes a bit of practice, but most parents catch on quickly *(see page 30)*. Start with five to seven infant-size diaper covers, depending on how frequently you do laundry.

Look for gussetted leg openings (to discourage leaks), a full Velcro panel in front for the best fit, and a trim, contoured design with not too much fabric between the legs.

Diaper liners

Diaper liners extend the absorbency of cloth diapers by adding another layer of cloth or paper. Liners are disposable, hourglass-shaped padded cotton or absorbent paper. Placed inside the diaper, they are especially useful at night, when traveling, or any time when it's difficult to change the baby frequently.

Diaper Disposal
Age: Birth–3 years

The days when your only choice was a smelly diaper pail with a cake of deodorant hanging in the lid are gone. Today

---

 PARENTS ALERT

Talcum powder: Never use powders containing talc. Breathing in talc can cause inhalation pneumonia in a child; in addition there are persistent—through unsubstantiated—reports of a link between talc and cancer. If you want to use a powder to dry your baby's rash, choose one that does not contain talc or cornstarch, which can exacerbate certain yeast infections. Never shake any powder directly onto your baby's bottom. Sprinkle it onto your hand first, and then rub it on your baby.

there are diaper disposal systems that lock in odors, usually by encasing the used diapers in a film of plastic. Here are the options.

Traditional diaper pail

For disposable or cloth diapers. This is simply a plastic pail with a lid, which you line with a plastic trash bag. Most diaper pails have a replaceable carbon filter in the lid to combat odors. Look for one with a pedal for hands-free use. This is the most economical type of diaper disposal, but the least effective for odor control—each time the lid is opened, the inevitable aroma escapes.

Plastic-film-cartridge pail

For disposable diapers. This type of pail is slim and cylindrical in shape, and contains a cartridge of scented plastic film that is twisted to encapsulate each diaper as it is added to the pail. When the pail is full, a blade on the lid cuts the film, leaving you with a long, sausage link-like string of wrapped diapers, which may then be disposed of in the trash. The best features of this system are its ease of use and its superior odor control. Its main drawback is its ecological insensitivity, since it adds an additional layer of plastic to each disposable diaper.

Plastic-bag-lined pail

For cloth or disposable diapers. The newest generation of diaper pails works on the same twist-away premise as the film-cartridge pail but uses ordinary plastic bags as liners. Although the odor-controlling ability is not quite as good, these pails combine convenience with the environmental benefits of using recycled bags if you choose.

Diapering Accessories
Age: Birth and up

Baby wipes

Although it's perfectly acceptable to use a wet washcloth to clean your baby during diaper changes, disposable baby wipes are more convenient. Ask your pediatrician whether you can begin using wipes as soon as you get home from the hospital. Most will allow unscented wipes as long as the baby has no adverse reactions. Some doctors recommend using damp washcloths or cotton balls to clean the baby for the first month or so.

There are many different brands of baby wipes on the market. Try a few to see which you like best. Most wipes come in scented and unscented versions, and many contain aloe, lanolin, or other additives meant to condition the baby's skin. These are not really necessary, and some babies may be allergic to them. Most brands are alcohol-free.

Look for thick, soft wipes that are neither too wet nor too dry. Quilting adds durability. To save money, buy generic brands (although the quality of these may not be great— shop around), buy in bulk, and buy refill packs rather than a new plastic container each time. It's also wise to buy one travel-sized container for your diaper bag, which can be re-filled from the regular box.

Wipe warmer

If using cool wipes upsets your baby, use this gadget to warm your wipes to a toasty temperature. There are two types of wipe warmer. The less expensive kind is like a heating pad that wraps around the box of wipes. The other is a hard plastic case that you transfer the wipes into. Both plug into a standard outlet.

Diaper ointments

Less is more when it comes to diaper ointments. For every-day use, all you really need is a barrier cream and a moisturizer. A barrier cream is just that—a barrier between the baby's skin and the wet diaper. Some parents like to apply a barrier cream like Balmex, Desitin, or A & D Ointment with every diaper change; others use it only if the skin looks irritated.

If your baby develops a diaper rash that doesn't respond to treatment with a barrier cream within 24 hours, consult your pediatrician. She may recommend a different over-the-counter treatment or prescribe a stronger medication.

Some babies have very dry skin, especially in the winter months. If your pediatrician suggests moisturizing, get a good-quality unscented lotion. Moisturizer can also be used for chapping on the face and as a light barrier in the diaper area.

Layette
Age: Birth–3 months

The layette is your baby's first wardrobe. It includes underwear, clothing, and sleepwear, as well as accessories like towels and blankets. In years past, expectant mothers often ordered complete preselected layettes from department stores. These are still available, but most women today opt to shop around. Building your layette yourself has several advantages. First, you get more style variety than if the entire layette is from one source. Also, you can tailor your layette to your own preferences and needs, eliminating items that you know you won't use or that you receive as gifts. Finally, babies outgrow their layettes so quickly that you may want to keep newborn-sized clothing to a minimum and save your money for larger-sized clothing that your baby can wear for a longer time.

If you don't plan to learn the sex of your baby through prenatal testing, don't buy a full layette before birth. Although some green and yellow (and blue and red) unisex items are fine, you'll probably want to fill in with some distinctly masculine or feminine styles once your baby has made an appearance. If you feel that you must purchase everything in advance, you may want to preselect both a boy's and a girl's layette from a store that will deliver the appropriate one to your home as soon as the baby is born.

Buy your layette items in newborn or three-month sizes, depending on the way the items are sized. Ignore advice to buy everything in six- or nine-month sizes—they will overwhelm your newborn. Instead, select only what you know you'll need for the first two or three months and fill in with larger sizes as your baby grows. Every baby's growth rate is different—yours may wear a six-month size at eight weeks . . . or at eight months. Another hint: save receipts and don't remove tags until your baby is born (with the exception of the outfit your baby will wear home from the hospital, which should be washed in advance and ready to go). You'll be glad you did this if you have either a preemie or a 10-pounder and everything has to be returned.

As you shop, look for clothing that, in addition to being adorable, will be practical and comfortable for your baby to wear.

Look for these:
- Soft, washable fabrics. Pure cotton is best unless you're buying flame-retardant sleepwear.
- Easy access to the diaper area.
- Snaps or zippers (buttons are awkward to fasten and present a choking hazard if they fall off).
- Wide or expandable neck openings.
- One-piece dressing (two-piece outfits tend to ride up and down on tiny babies).
- Socks and booties with gentle elastic at the ankle.

And avoid these:
- Strings or ribbons, which can pose a strangulation hazard. Get nightgowns and hoods with elastic instead.
- Rough seams.
- Anything that needs to be ironed.
- Dresses (impractical and unflattering on a floppy newborn).
- Stiff clothing like denim jeans or overalls with hardware.
- Shoes (inappropriate for infants).

The following is a list of recommended items for a basic layette. You'll notice that this list differs from those provided by stores or clothing manufacturers. That's because such

FLAME-RETARDANT SLEEPWEAR

Deciding whether or not to use flame-retardant sleepwear is an individual choice. The label "flame-retardant" does not guarantee that a fabric will not burn, only that it will stop burning immediately when not exposed to a direct flame. Polyester, nylon, and acrylic are inherently flame-retardant, so the flame-retardant qualities cannot wash out. (It is, however, important to follow the care instructions on the garment's label, as certain ingredients in laundry products can interfere with the effectiveness of the flame retardant.)

Most cotton is not flame-retardant. However, many parents prefer to dress their infants in cotton clothing all the time because it feels, looks, and washes better than polyester or other synthetics. In 1998, the CPSC amended the sleepwear standards to permit the sale of cotton sleepwear for children as long as it was snug-fitting.

A good compromise may be to use flame-retardant garments at night when you cannot keep constant watch over your baby. Another, albeit pricey, option is the new flame-retardant cottons. If you use these, choose naturally flame-retardant compacted cotton rather than cotton treated with flame-retardant chemicals. (You can use soap flakes on compacted cotton, but not on treated cotton; read the label carefully to be sure.)

companies would often have you buy more than you need or omit items they don't carry. Before you go shopping, check off any items that you know you will be receiving as gifts or hand-me-downs. Also consider how often you plan to do laundry, and buy accordingly. Be aware of the season and the climate you live in, too. A May baby, for example, doesn't need a snowsuit (unless you live in Alaska)—a fleece blanket or sweater and hat will suffice for chilly spring days. Likewise, keep short-sleeved rompers to a bare minimum for a late-August arrival, unless you live in a place where it's warm year round.

Undershirts (8–10)

Undershirts are the foundation of your baby's wardrobe—he'll probably wear at least one a day at first, either alone or under clothes.

There are several varieties:
- *Bodysuits or Onesies.* These are pulled on over your baby's head. They snap at the crotch, so they can't ride up. Some parents prefer not to use these until the umbilical cord stump heals, but soft cotton ones should be fine from day one.
- *Pullovers.* These have lapped shoulders and are smooth and comfortable.
- *Side-snap shirts.* These eliminate having to pull a shirt over the baby's head, which is especially helpful on brand-new babies. Some have snaps attached to fabric tabs so that the metal never touches the baby's skin.
- *Side-tie shirts.* These are lumpy and tend to come untied easily but are an alternative to metal snaps.

Sleepers or stretchies (4–8)

Newborn babies spend most of their time sleeping, so they spend a lot of time in their pajamas. Choosing stretchies with feet avoids the problem of lost socks or booties.

Nightgowns (1–4)

Formerly known as drawstring gowns, these full-length gowns now have elastic at the bottom. Start with one to see if you like them—some parents don't because they tend to ride up. Others like them for nighttime because they provide the easiest access for diaper changes.

Blanket sleepers (2–4)

For late-fall or winter babies. These zip-up footed sleepers are made of warm polyester fleece and can be used over an

Swaddling Steps

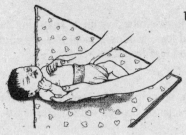

1. Fold a receiving blanket into a triangle and place your baby in the center so that his neck rests at the top of the largest side.

2. Pull one corner across his shoulder and tuck it in below his other arm and underneath his bottom.

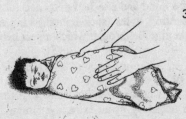

3. Repeat step 2 with the opposite corner. Then, gather the open folds at the bottom and tuck the blanket underneath your baby to cover his feet.

undershirt or a stretchy. Blanket sleepers also come in a bunting or sleeping-bag style, without legs.

Rompers (3–6)

These are one-piece "play clothes" with a snap crotch. Choose long sleeves and legs, with or without feet, for cold weather, short sleeves and legs for warm weather.

Socks or booties (4–8)

Fewer for warm weather, more for colder weather. Look for stretch-terry newborn socks or booties with gentle elastic cuffs.

Sweaters (1–2)

Cardigans are most practical. Just one in light cotton for summer babies. In colder weather, it's nice to have two— one light cotton or cotton fleece (sweatshirt material) and one heavier cotton polar fleece, acrylic, or soft wool.

Hats (1–3)

For summer, a lightweight cotton sun hat with a brim is best. For warmth, use light cotton knit caps indoors and heavy cotton, polar fleece, or acrylic that covers the ears for outdoors.

Snowsuit or bunting (1)

For winter babies. Soft, warm polar fleece is the best snowsuit choice for a newborn, who doesn't require a water-repellent shell. Look for a hood and attached mitts and foot coverings. Make sure bunting styles (sack bottom) have a slit near the bottom in the middle through which a seat belt can fit.

Receiving blankets (4–6)

These small square blankets have dozens of uses. Use for swaddling the baby (see page 39), as an extra layer in cold weather, for covering the baby in the stroller or bassinet, as a play mat on the floor, and more. Good receiving blanket

DRESSING FOR THE WEATHER

By the time a baby's inner thermostat has regulated itself—usually by around six months—you can use your own comfort as a guide for dressing your baby. The adage that a newborn always needs one more layer than an adult is untrue, but very young babies do need some bundling when the weather is cold. A newborn should wear a hat even when the weather is only slightly cool, because a significant amount of body heat is lost through the head. When it's really cold, the hat should cover the ears, and hands and feet should be well covered, too.

Use common sense when dressing your baby for the elements. If your baby is perspiring, it means he's overheated. If his arms or thighs feel cool, he may be chilly (hands and feet tend to be cool all the time). On a hot summer day he will be most comfortable in a short-sleeved outfit that doesn't cover the legs. On warm nights, put him to bed in a lightweight footed sleeper or cover him with a light blanket.

In cooler weather, dressing a baby in layers makes sense, because you can add and subtract clothing when you move from the frosty outdoors to a heated house or car. Always remove the baby's hat and at least one layer of clothing (or unzip his snowsuit) in the car to avoid overheating.

fabrics are cotton thermal knit, cotton jersey, cotton flannel, and polar fleece for cold weather.

Hooded towels (2–4)
Choose soft cotton terry cloth. Avoid appliqués, which could scratch skin or unravel.

Washcloths (4–6)
Although any washcloth will do, those for babies are smaller and softer—and easier to use.

Bibs (1–2)

Don't buy too many bibs to start with, because if your baby doesn't spit up or drool a lot, you won't need them until he starts eating solid food. Choose small "drool bibs" for a newborn.

Diapers

Your baby will go through 10 to 12 diapers a day during his first months, so buy accordingly. If you're laundering your own cloth diapers, start with two to five dozen.

Cloth diapers (one dozen)

Even if you're using disposable diapers, you'll need some cloth diapers to protect your shoulders when burping the baby, to protect sheets from spit-up, to wipe the baby's face, to clean up spills, and for lots of other uses.

Diaper covers (5–7)

If you will be using cloth diapers and your diaper service doesn't provide them.

Everyday Clothes

Play Clothes

These are the outfits your child will wear most of his waking hours and those he will be seen in most often. First and foremost, your baby's play clothes should be comfortable. As with layette items, look for soft fabrics, smooth seams, and a good fit. Another important consideration is ease of dressing—for you at first and for your child too as he grows toward toddlerhood. Your baby's everyday outfits should also be completely washable and should not require any additional upkeep such as line drying or ironing. Look for sturdy preshrunk cottons or cotton/polyester blends. Blends shrink and wrinkle less than 100-percent cotton, but they stain and pill more easily and probably won't wear as well.

As for appearance, what you choose will be a reflection of your own personal style, and later, increasingly, of your child's. And of course affordability plays a big part in deciding what, and how much, to buy for your child. But whether your baby sports overalls and T-shirts, chintz dresses, dinosaur-print rompers, khakis and oxford-cloth shirts, or denim and leather, make sure that what he's wearing is appropriate for his age and stage.

Play clothes for infants and babies

As your baby outgrows his layette items, replace his tiny stretchies with clothing in six- or nine-month sizes (some babies grow so quickly, they can jump right to a 12-month size). For the first year, look for one-piece rompers, soft overalls, long- and short-sleeved T-shirts (bodysuit styles stay tucked in) with snaps at the neck, cotton knit dresses and jumpers, elastic-waist pants (sweatpant styles work well), and cardigan sweaters and sweatshirts. Many parents prefer the ease and simplicity of one-piece dressing, while others relish outfitting their offspring in multipiece ensembles. If you don't go the one-piece route, be aware that young babies tend to come untucked easily, so it's wise to anchor the outfit with a bodysuit.

Avoid anything that might cause discomfort or pose a safety hazard, such as heavy zippers and hardware, belts, tight elastic, scratchy lace, buttons or trim that could be pulled or chewed off, ribbons, and drawstrings. Also, pass up any outfit that doesn't have adequate access to the diaper area—you'd be surprised at how many infant clothes do not. Finally, when your baby starts pulling himself up (usually at seven to nine months), put away outfits with feet unless they have nonskid soles.

Babies under a year old tend to stay relatively clean (as long as large bibs and well-fitting diapers are used), so you may not have to wash your baby's outfit every time he wears it. Factor in that babies this age grow very quickly—they're often in and out of a size in a month or two—and you'll probably want to focus more on quality than quantity of play clothes right now.

Play clothes for one-year-olds

Much of the advice about dressing infants also applies to one-year-olds, but as your baby becomes a toddler, he will also have some different sartorial needs. Although it's still a good idea to keep your toddler's play clothes soft and comfortable, your sturdy walker can now handle more constructed clothing like pants with zipper flies (until your child is out of diapers and will be pulling his pants up and down himself), dresses with waistbands, skirts, belts, and suspenders. Overalls and jumpers with adjustable straps are great for this age, as are knit pants with roll-down cuffs or elastic-waist woven pants that can be rolled up. Bodysuits are still great for covering the diaper (especially under a dress) and keeping everything tucked in.

As your baby's growth slows and he becomes harder on his clothes, look for sturdy garments that will last an entire season, or maybe even more. Now is the time to buy more outfits, because a one-year-old is bound to get dirty. At this stage, you may want to buy a few nice special-occasion outfits and look for more bargain-priced everyday clothing.

Play clothes for two-year-olds

You will probably dress your two-year-old similarly to the way you dressed your one-year-old. The big difference this year is the emergence of self-dressing and possibly toilet-teaching. Look for clothing that is easy for your child to put on and take off. Instead of snap-crotch one-piece outfits and overalls, buy elastic-waist pants and skirts, and shirts and dresses with large neckbands. Avoid buttons (although some children this age can handle large ones), zippers (which can pinch skin), and anything that takes a lot of fine-motor coordination to fasten. If you plan to let your child choose his own outfits, stick to solid colors in one family (primaries, pastels, earth tones) or simple patterns that coordinate with each other (all solid bottoms and patterned or printed tops work well). Also, choose clothes with a clearly marked front and back (a picture or pocket on the front, for example) or teach your child that the tag goes in the back.

Two-year-olds are tough on their clothes. Choose play clothes that will stand up to a lot of washes and will not break your heart—or your bank account—if they get ruined.

Sleepwear

Since your child will spend about half of his life in bed as a baby and toddler, he'll need a full wardrobe of sleepwear to get him through this stage. Pajamas should be soft, stretchy, comfortable, and completely free of ornamentation. They should be either flame-retardant or snug-fitting cotton (*see page 37*). Look for easy diaper access, feet with nonskid soles for babies over six months, well-attached snaps, and plastic rather than metal zippers.

Winter pajamas should be made of a warm fabric such as acrylic fleece or heavy polyester or cotton knit. If your baby doesn't like to sleep under a blanket, you may want to layer a blanket sleeper or fleece pajamas over thinner cotton ones.

In warm weather, look for lighter-weight cottons and polyesters with short sleeves and pants (unless your house is heavily air conditioned). Girls can wear thin nightgowns, but avoid elasticized sleeves, which can be uncomfortable.

Tiny bathrobes and kimonos may look adorable, but most young children have little occasion or desire to wear them. Slippers, on the other hand, are a must if your toddler will be walking on chilly floors. Look for nonskid soles sewn onto soft uppers of fabric, leather, fleece, cotton knit, felt, or boiled wool. Stay away from plush animal slippers for toddlers—they're bulky and easy to trip over.

Underwear

As long as your baby is in diapers, a bodysuit-style undershirt is the only undergarment he will need. Onesies are available in short- and long-sleeved styles as well as thermal knit, so every season is covered. Underwear is available at all prices. The difference between the discount store pack and the imported French version is the quality of the cotton—the higher the thread count, the softer it will be.

If you live in a very cold climate, you may also want to use long underwear. Whether you choose one-piece union suits or two-piece sets, make sure the underwear is soft, absorbent cotton knit with a snug fit and easy diaper access.

Many children will start toilet-teaching during their second year. This is the time to pack away the onesies and move on to T-shirt or tank-style undershirts.

Like diapers, training pants can be cloth or disposable. If you use cloth training pants, look for styles with extra padding in the crotch. Underpants for both boys and girls should be soft, absorbent cotton knit. Look for styles with encased elastic or band legs if your child's skin is easily irritated. Once your child is wearing underpants regularly, invest in 12 to 15 pairs. Also be aware that children often wear a larger underwear size than their regular clothing (mostly because underwear tends to shrink so much).

Special-Occasion Clothes

These are the few "fancy" clothes that your baby will wear for special ceremonies (like his christening or naming), holidays, and parties. For girls this probably means a dainty dress, while baby boys look smart in outfits made of special fabrics like velour, linen, knit silk, or even cashmere. Look for high quality, since you won't need many of these.

Special-occasion clothes for infants and babies

For infants, simple is always better. Unless your baby is wearing a ceremonial outfit like an heirloom christening gown, stay away from decoration and ornamentation just as you would when choosing play clothes. For girls, a soft cotton knit, velour, or rayon dress is flattering and practical. Team it with a bodysuit or diaper cover, and pretty socks or a tiny pair of tights if the weather is cool. In summer, a breezy cotton bubble (blousey snap-crotch sunsuit) is also adorable.

Don't outfit your baby boy in a miniature blazer and tie—he can't carry it off and the tie is a choking hazard. Instead, opt for a simple one- or two-piece outfit in a dressy fabric. Cashmere, velour, and soft merino wool are good choices when it's cool. Pima cotton, linen, and washable knit silk look great in spring and summer. Hand-knit items like cardigans and even whole sweater outfits are also charming and special.

Special-occasion clothes for one- and two-year-olds

Older babies and toddlers still look adorable in simple, soft outfits made of luxurious fabrics. But once a baby is upright, he is also able to move on to more sophisticated special-occasion styles. Girls can now wear dresses that have more ornamentation—smocking, appliqués (make sure they are securely attached), and ruffles are all classics. Avoid stiff lace, which can be scratchy.

Boys this age look cute in corduroy or velour overalls, khakis, hand-knit sweaters or sweater vests, button-down shirts, and (lined) wool shorts or pants. If you're partial to the English style of dressing little boys—sailor suits, Peter Pan collars, knickers, and knee socks—be prepared for embarrassed groans from your son a few years down the line.

Footwear

Footwear for infants and babies

For the first three to twelve months of his life, the only footwear your baby really needs is socks. Shoes are unnecessary for babies until they learn to walk: they are cumbersome and heavy and can interfere with learning to walk unless they are professionally fitted and specifically designated as first walkers. Booties and soft "shoes" are usually just decorative, but they can be useful for keeping feet warm in cold weather and providing traction for a baby who's learning to stand and cruise. Choose soft-soled booties made of soft cloth or leather moccasin styles. Lace-up booties (the ones that look like little sneakers, for example) may deter a baby who is constantly pulling his socks off. Look for breathable cotton or cotton/spandex blend socks with cuffs or gentle elastic to keep them on. Nonskid soles are useful for standing babies. Buy eight to ten pairs of socks, and retire them when they become threadbare or too snug.

Footwear for toddlers

As soon as your baby takes his first steps, it's time to buy him his first pair of shoes. First shoes should have soles that are nonslip (not smooth leather) and flexible. Uppers should be flexible, too, and breathable (leather or canvas is a good choice). Buy shoes with a low cut—in the past, it was thought that new walkers needed high-cut shoes for ankle support, but now experts agree that low-top styles promote better ankle development. The counter (back of the shoe behind the heel) should be firm, and the top should be padded or bound with fabric. The toe box should be wide and gently rounded. It's also very important that first shoes—indeed, all shoes for growing feet—fit well. Resist the temptation to buy shoes at a discount store or through a catalogue. Instead, bring your baby to a shoe store with a good reputation for fitting children. To ensure a proper fit, have your child wear the type of socks he will be wearing with the shoes.

Check the fit of your child's shoes often because babies outgrow shoes quickly—usually in two to three months. Shoes should be good quality, but it's not so important that they be extremely durable, since your baby will probably outgrow them before wearing them out.

Your baby's first shoes will probably be sneakers or oxfords designed for new walkers. As he grows, he'll probably build a wider shoe wardrobe.

DRESSING MULTIPLES

Although you definitely can't dress two babies for the price of one, you won't have to buy everything in duplicate (or triplicate), either. Unless you're intent on dressing your babies identically or your children wear different sizes, one large layette will suffice if you're willing to do a lot of laundry. When shopping for a layette for your multiples, stock up on basics like undershirts, socks, and stretchies. To simplify shopping, consider buying the same styles in two or more colors or patterns. This also gives the babies a coordinated, though not identical, look, which you may like.

You will need to buy each child his own sweater, jacket, snowsuit, winter hat, sun hat, bathing suit, and, once they start walking, shoes. It is not recommended for children to share shoes, since shoes mold to each individual's foot shape.

As your children grow—very likely at different rates—sharing clothes will probably become less practical. By age two or so, boys and girls will probably need their own wardrobes. Identical and same-size, same-sex fraternal multiples can share for as long as they are willing. (Don't be surprised if they go through a phase of wanting to be dressed identically around age three, even if you've never encouraged it.)

Some stores and catalogues offer discounts for multiples, so be sure to ask. There are several catalogues and Web sites that specialize in clothing for multiples. *(See the shopping resources on pages 215–216 for a list of these.)*

Here are some shoe-buying guidelines:
- *Sandals.* Sandals for babies and toddlers should have a closed heel rather than just a strap in the back. Look for supportive styles with wide straps, like fishermen's sandals. Never put a baby or toddler in clogs, mules,

thongs, or strappy sandals, as they can cause him to
trip.

- *Boots.* Plastic or rubber rain boots should be worn
  only outside, since waterproof material makes for
  sweaty feet. Snow boots should be insulated and fit
  snugly for maximum warmth. Do not purchase
  heavy-soled hiking boots or cowboy boots for a
  young child.
- *Party shoes.* They're fancy, they're shiny, and little
  girls love them. Unfortunately, those beautiful Mary
  Janes tend to be made out of stiff, sticky vinyl (real
  patent leather is quite pricey). Such shoes should be
  worn infrequently. Better yet, opt for a sturdier party
  shoe of nubuck or smooth leather in a cross-strap or
  T-strap style.
- *Sneakers.* Look for flexible styles specifically made
  for new walkers. Heavy, thick-soled, or high-top ath-
  letic styles are not appropriate for toddling feet.
- *Water shoes.* Also known as aqua socks, these shoes
  have rubber bottoms and nylon and mesh uppers. Water shoes are comfortable, dry quickly, and are great
  protection for little feet at the beach or pool.

Seasonal Dressing

Summer

In the summer, all your baby really needs is a swim diaper, a
sun hat, and a sunscreen with an SPF of at least 15.

Swim diapers come in two types: disposable and cloth.
Disposable swim diapers are constructed like pull-ups,
with tear-away sides, and are brightly colored. They do not
expand in the water like regular disposable diapers, so they
are more comfortable for the baby and more hygienic for
the pool. Cloth swim diapers come in several varieties.
One kind consists of two-layer pants with polypropylene-
backed nylon or cotton on the outside and soft knit on the
inside. Another style is polyester mesh-lined nylon with

terry-cloth padding between the legs. Swim diapers can be worn alone or under a bathing suit. Some bathing suits have built-in swim diapers, which necessitates a complete change if they get dirty (be sure you have a backup if you choose this style). Swim diapers are worn instead of regular diapers; they will contain solid waste but not urine, so they should not be substituted for regular diapers except in the water.

Children's bathing suits come in every style and fabric imaginable. It's better to opt for quick-drying nylon rather than soggy cotton. Avoid girls' styles with thin straps, which can cut into skin and cause discomfort. If your child is very sensitive to the sun, you might want to try a wetsuit rather than a bathing suit. These nylon/spandex suits zip up the front and protect the wearer's shoulders, torso, and upper legs.

Along with sunscreen, a light-colored cotton T-shirt is a good après-swim coverup, though some parents prefer the greater coverage of a hooded terry-cloth robe (choose zip or button front rather than wraparound for safety and convenience). Sun hats should shade the back of the neck as well as the ears and face—look for wide-brimmed or safari styles.

Fall

Transitional dressing can be tricky, so it's best to use the layered look in the fall. Dress your baby or toddler in a short-sleeved undershirt under a long-sleeved top (make sure turtlenecks have snaps or very stretchy neck openings). You can then add a sweater, sweatshirt, or jacket if the temperature dips. Acrylic fleece is a wonderful fabric for fall jackets—it's soft and cozy, yet won't cause overheating. Clothing with Velcro, snaps, and plastic zippers is easier to put on and take off than clothes with buttons.

Babies under one year should wear a hat or a hood even when the weather is only slightly cool or breezy. Hats should cover the ears and fit snugly, but not too tightly.

Winter
Winter dressing for infants and babies

Babies under one year old should be dressed especially warmly in cold weather, because they usually don't move around enough to raise their body temperatures. Buy a quilted or fleece snowsuit with a hood and hand and foot coverings in a size that will last through the entire season. Do not buy a sack-type snowsuit for babies over three months old (unless it converts into one with legs) because your baby will want more freedom of movement. Look for a snowsuit with a full zippered front for quick and easy changes. A nylon or water-resistant outer layer makes the snowsuit stiffer and heavier, and is not necessary unless your baby will routinely be out in wet conditions.

In addition to the hood, get your baby a warm cotton, acrylic, or fleece hat that covers his ears and forehead. Scarves are inappropriate for babies and small children, as are boots for nonwalkers. Optimally, the snowsuit will have flaps that fold over to protect the hands and feet. If you must purchase mittens, thumbless ones will be much easier to put on. Attach them to the cuffs of the snowsuit with clips rather than a string.

Winter dressing for toddlers

The type of winter gear your toddler needs depends not only on the climate, but also on your lifestyle. A city tot who spends a lot of his time in the stroller will need a warm snowsuit to protect him from the elements. A suburban child who goes from house to car to mall is probably better off with a winter jacket and separate waterproof pants for playing in the snow. Look for well-insulated jackets and snowsuits with a water-resistant nylon outer layer and a fleece, down, or Thinsulate lining for warmth. A snowsuit should have a full zipper down the front, and cuffs at the wrist and ankle. Jackets should be cuffed at the wrist and waistband. Parkas should have elastic at the waist and cover the seat. Do not choose a wool coat for everyday wear—it's too heavy, can be itchy, and will smell if it gets wet.

Spring
Spring dressing for infants and babies

Like fall, spring is a transitional time when dressing your baby in layers is the best bet. Cotton sweaters and snap-front jackets made of cotton or acrylic fleece are wonderful choices for spring outerwear. If you live in a place where it rains a lot in the spring, a water-resistant nylon jacket with a hood is also useful. Avoid nonbreathable vinyl or rubber slickers for small babies. And don't forget to keep a hat on your baby's head until temperatures are in the sixties.

Spring dressing for toddlers

For many toddlers, spring means splashing around in slush and rain puddles. Let your child puddle jump to his heart's content in a waterproof coat with a hood or hat. Vinyl or rubber slickers provide the most protection—just make sure they have plenty of ventilation so your child doesn't get overheated. Look for grommeted air holes under the arms and a mesh panel under a flap in the back. Snaps or zippers are easier to fasten and unfasten than buttons or the traditional "fireman" raincoat clips. If your child is a real water lover, you may want to invest in a pair of rain pants, too.

Accessories

There is no end to the adorable accessories available for babies and toddlers: tiny hair ornaments, mini backpacks and pocketbooks, charming hats. There are even lines of jewelry made especially for baby girls. Accessories are completely optional and just for fun (with the exception of protective hats). Follow common sense when buying.

Jewelry

Don't put anything on your baby that could pose a choking hazard, including beaded jewelry that could be pulled or chewed apart. Earrings for pierced ears should have surgical

DETERMINING THE RIGHT SIZE

Sizing on children's clothing varies drastically from manufacturer to manufacturer, so it takes some experience—and some trial and error—before you can buy with confidence. The old rule of thumb for baby clothing up to 24-month size was to double the age of the child. This still works for some brands if your baby is of average size. However, European baby clothes, higher-end designer clothes, and those from chain stores like babyGap, Gymboree, and the Children's Place tend to be sized to match the baby's true age (for an average-size baby).

All catalogues and online stores, many stores, and some manufacturers supply a sizing chart with which you can determine your baby's size according to his height and weight. This is helpful, though by no means foolproof. The best rule of thumb is to learn to eyeball an outfit and make a good guess as to which size to buy. This becomes easier with experience and as your child grows older and his growth rate slows. Until then, save receipts, and always include a gift receipt when giving a gift (and hope others will do the same for you).

steel posts and screw-on backs that cannot loosen or be pulled off. Before piercing a child's ears, parents may want to consult with their pediatrician.

Hair ornaments
Choose soft headbands or fabric-covered ponytail holders rather than clips, barrettes, or rubber bands. Some babies don't like having anything around their heads.

Backpacks and purses
These should be small and light enough for the child to carry comfortably, and not have long straps or strings that could pose a strangulation hazard.

HOW TO GET THE BEST FOR LESS

Dressing a baby can cost big money, but with a little creativity and legwork, you can outfit your child in good-quality, stylish clothes for below-retail price. Here are some tips from the pros:

- *Shop often.* Big chains like Gap, Old Navy, Gymboree, and the Children's Place have great sales, but marked-down items sell quickly. Check in every couple of weeks to see what has been reduced. Better yet, find out what day of the week they do their markdowns, and schedule your shopping accordingly.
- *Shop early.* A year early, that is. End-of-season clearance sales are the best, with prices often 50 to 70 percent off. As soon as you're confident at predicting what size your child will be the next year, take advantage of these great sales.
- *Shop off-price.* Off-price stores like Marshalls, T.J. Maxx, Baby Depot, and Daffy's have great deals on children's clothes. They often have high-end designer items for up to 70 percent off and low prices on basics like socks and underwear. The secret to shopping at these stores is knowing the value of the items—there's a lot of junk mixed in with the good labels and selling at similar prices.
- *Shop outlets.* Manufacturers' outlets often, although not always, offer significant discounts. An advantage to outlets is that they tend to carry a designer's entire line, rather than the bits and pieces you find at off-price retailers. Outlets can have excellent end-of-season sales, too. Again, it's good to know what the item you're buying sells for at retail, so you'll know if you're getting a real savings.
- *Shop consignment.* Consignment stores are a treasure trove of gently used, and sometimes completely new, children's clothing at remarkably low prices. Good consignment

---

HOW TO GET THE BEST FOR LESS
(continued)

---

stores won't accept stained or used-looking clothes—
find one in your area that has high standards. Many
people consign unused clothes that didn't fit during the
right season or that their child never had the occasion to
wear. Consignment stores are a particularly good
source for special-occasion clothes like fancy dresses,
blazers, and wool dress coats.

- *Shop judiciously.* There's no reason everything your
baby wears has to be top-of-the-line. Large discount
chains like Babies "R" Us, Kids "R" Us, Kmart, Wal-
Mart, and Target offer great prices on the basics and
often feature their own line of decent-quality cotton
clothing. Look for undershirts, socks, packaged layette
items, cotton T-shirts, pajamas, towels, and crib sheets
at these stores.

- *Shop online.* Almost every children's clothing catalogue
and many retail stores now have Web sites that offer
marked-down items. Check your favorite Web sites regularly, as sale items sometimes change daily, and quantities tend to be limited.

Sunglasses

Children's sunglasses should fit comfortably and have plastic lenses that provide 100-percent protection from UV rays.
If your child doesn't want to wear sunglasses, don't force
him. Never attach sunglasses to a child's face with straps or
strings.

Chapter 3

Feeding

Feeding your baby for the first three years will be a continuing challenge. From the days (and nights) of leaky breasts or endless bottles to sterilize, to faces smeared with strained peas and floors decorated with crushed pretzels, equipping yourself with the right gear can make this essential baby-care duty a lot easier—and even fun.

There are many gizmos and gadgets available to aid in breast-, bottle-, and table feeding. Some—like a breast pump, electric bottle warmer with refrigerated compartment, and spill-proof toddler cup—will make your life infinitely easier. Others may be nice to have but are not essential. This chapter presents all the feeding-related baby gear, with descriptions that will help you decide what you need and what you don't.

Breast-Feeding

If you plan to breast-feed your baby exclusively, you already have most of the equipment you need. There are some accessories, however, that will make breast-feeding easier, especially if you plan to go back to work or leave your baby for extended periods of time.

Nursing bra

Nursing bras have a flap on each cup that folds down for nursing. There are many different styles of fasteners—hooks, snaps, clips, even special folds. Try them to see which you find the most comfortable and convenient. It may seem to make sense to buy nursing bras as your bustline expands during pregnancy, but it's a good idea to put off this purchase until near the end of your pregnancy. Keep in mind that you will probably go through three or four bra sizes before arriving at the size you'll be when you're nursing. Wait until your eighth month to buy nursing bras, and then buy only two or three, since you still don't know just what size you'll need after giving birth. Nursing bras should be very supportive, and either cotton or cotton-lined for absorbency. You may also want to buy a couple of sleep bras, which are unconstructed cotton nursing bras to wear at night. Many women find these comfortable, especially during engorgement, when breasts are extra tender and leaky.

Nursing pads

These are small round pads to place in your bra to protect your clothing from leaking colostrum or milk. Disposable nursing pads are made of several layers of thin, absorbent paper backed by a plastic liner. Cloth nursing pads are made of absorbent cotton, and, though thicker, may be more comfortable and economical. Buy one set or box of nursing pads before your baby is born, as you will probably start leaking colostrum in the hospital. Wait before buying more, because many women find that leaking is not a problem after the first few weeks of nursing.

Nursing clothes

Nursing nightgowns, tops, and dresses have hidden slits in the front that open for discreet nursing. Nursing nightgowns are convenient, but be sure to try before you buy—some have slits that hang open and provide much more exposure than you want. Regular nightgowns or pajama tops that button down the front also provide quick and easy nursing access.

The slits on nursing shirts and dresses are usually much more camouflaged and often have fasteners. Don't buy too many nursing shirts at the beginning, because you may find that you prefer simply to push up the bottom of your shirt or unbutton it and throw a receiving blanket over your shoulder.

Nursing pillow

A nursing pillow is a firm cushion that supports your back, arms, and neck while you nurse. One kind is U-shaped and wraps around your body to support your arms, which in turn support the baby at the correct level for nursing. Another kind is wedge-shaped. Nursing pillows are wonderful for nursing newborns, who do not have the strength to hold themselves in the nursing position. A nursing pillow is especially useful after a cesarean delivery, because it keeps the weight of the baby off the incision.

Nursing pillows come in several different styles and with different features. Look for a padded strap that wraps around your waist and supports your lower back; a removable, washable cover; and an accessory pocket. Inflatable models are great for travel.

If you plan to nurse twins together, get a twin nursing pillow. This larger pillow has more space on the sides and straps around you to keep it in place.

Nursing stool

This small angled footstool is meant to eliminate neck, arm, and shoulder strain while nursing. When you place your feet on the stool, your lap is elevated into a position that may be more comfortable for breast-feeding. Most hospitals have these, so you may be able to try one out before you come home to see if it's comfortable for you.

Nursing shawl

An alternative to the receiving blanket draped across the chest, this large cotton "bib" attaches around the mother's neck and covers the nursing baby. Many nursing shawls have a stiff neckline that stands away from your body so you can look down and see the baby. This opening also provides ventilation. If you plan to use one of these, get your baby used to it early, or she may refuse to nurse covered up when you introduce it.

Breast Pumps

Breast pumps are invaluable for nursing mothers who need or want to spend time away from their babies, or who want other caregivers to be able to feed the baby. Regular pumping with an efficient pump should also keep your milk production at a full-time nursing level. Occasional pumping allows you to leave your baby for a few hours at a time without worrying about leaking and the discomfort of missing feedings. The type of pump you choose depends on how long and how often you plan to pump.

Manual pump

A manual pump may be a good choice if you plan to pump infrequently. These small, hand-powered pumps are portable, inexpensive ($10–$50), and easy to use. They are not as efficient as electric pumps, however, and many women find that they cannot pump a full feeding with a hand pump. Even if you don't plan on giving your baby any bottles, you may want to have a manual pump available to relieve engorgement.

There are two types of manual pumps, syringe and trigger. Syringe pumps consist of two cylinders that fit together and are attached to a collection bottle. The end of the smaller cylinder is placed against the nipple, and the other cylinder is moved back and forth to create suction and draw

Portable Piston Electric Pump

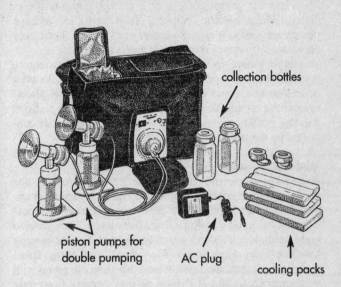

collection bottles

piston pumps for double pumping

AC plug

cooling packs

Hand Pump

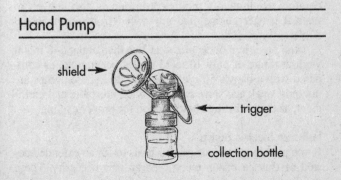

shield →

← trigger

← collection bottle

out the milk. Some syringe pumps allow you to adjust the
pressure, and therefore the speed and comfort of pumping.
Many electric pumps come with a syringe pump to use in
places where electric pumping isn't possible. Syringe
pumps are small, inexpensive, and easy to use. Their only
drawback is that they require two hands to operate.

Trigger pumps are even easier to use because they require
only one hand to operate. The trigger mechanism fits on a
collection bottle and is attached to a shield that is placed
against the nipple. You then squeeze the trigger in and out,
creating gentle suction to express the milk. Pressure is controlled by the rate at which you pump.

Mini electric pump

Powered by an electric outlet or batteries, these small pumps
mimic a baby's sucking motion by creating suction in cycles. Mini electric pumps are great for expressing the occasional bottle to leave with Dad or a baby-sitter. They are also
highly portable, allowing you to easily stick to your nursing
schedule even when you're away from your baby. These
pumps are not practical for mothers who need to pump with
maximum speed and efficiency, as they express from only
one breast at a time and may not be strong enough to empty
both breasts on a regular basis.

Look for a mini electric pump that automatically works at
50 cycles per minute and has adjustable vacuum controls for
comfort. High-quality mini electric pumps also convert to
manual trigger pumps, and are priced from about $60 to
$150.

Mini electric models priced at less than about $40 might
work at a rate of only 10 to 15 cycles per minute, as com-
pared with a baby's 50 cycles per minute. These pumps are
not only weak and slow, but often uncomfortable and ineffi-
cient, as they substitute hard suction for proper cycling.

Full-size electric pump

If you plan to pump on a regular basis or for an extended period of time, a piston electric pump is a necessity. These

state-of-the-art machines automatically work at 50 cycles per minute, closely mimicking a baby's natural sucking action. Full-size electric pumps allow you to pump both breasts at once, often making it possible to express 8 to 10 ounces of milk in 10 to 15 minutes. Because piston pumps use cycling rather than hard suction to draw out the milk, they are very comfortable—sometimes more so than a suckling baby.

Until recently, most women rented piston pumps from hospital supply stores for about $30 per month. These hospital pumps, which retail at about $1,200, are heavy and difficult to transport, but they offered the most comfortable and efficient way to collect milk. Many working mothers leave a hospital pump at their offices, to avoid having to lug it back and forth every day. If you only plan to pump for a few months, it may still make sense to rent a pump. Remember to factor in the cost of buying an accessory kit (nipple shields, tubing, bottles), which doesn't come with the pump.

Now, for about a quarter of the price of a hospital pump ($150–$275), you can buy a portable piston electric pump. These pumps work on the same principle as the hospital pump; they just aren't manufactured to withstand years of constant use (good ones are fully warrantied for two years). These lightweight pumps come with a carrying case that includes an insulated cooler section for milk storage, cooling packs, collection bottles, and tubing. You can even buy an adapter that hooks up to the lighter in your car.

Weigh the price of a portable piston pump against the approximate $30 a month you'll spend to rent a pump plus $40 to $50 to purchase the pumping accessories. If you plan to pump for more than six months, plan to have another child, or just want the convenience of a portable pump, this is a worthwhile investment.

Breast Milk Storage
Breast milk can be stored in the refrigerator in the bottle it's collected in or in a baby bottle. For longer-term storage, freeze the milk in plastic bags. Disposable bottle liners,

BREAST MILK STORAGE GUIDE

Breast milk may be stored safely following these guidelines:

At room temperature (66–72°F)	**4 hours**
In refrigerator (34–40°F)	**48 hours**
In freezer compartment of refrigerator (20–28°F)	**2 weeks**
In separate freezer (5–15°F)	**3 months**
In deep freezer (0°F)	**6 months**

heavy-duty zip-top freezer bags, and special milk collection bags are all appropriate. Bags manufactured specifically for breast milk storage are stronger but more expensive than standard disposable bottle liners. Both have ounce measurements printed on the side. If you use regular food storage bags, note how much milk you pumped from the bottle you collected it in, and then mark the amount on the bag before you freeze it.

Bottle-Feeding

Bottles

If you plan to feed your baby with conventional bottles, you will need about four 4-ounce bottles and ten to twelve 8-ounce bottles. If you use disposables (reusable holders with disposable liners), start with two 4-ounce holders, four 8-ounce holders, and a box of 100 or more liners in each size. Cut the numbers in half if you will be using the bottles to supplement breast-feeding.

Bottles come in a dizzying array of shapes, sizes, styles, and patterns. There are benefits and drawbacks to each.

Open only a few of those you've bought before your baby's birth in case she doesn't like the one you've chosen.

Opaque plastic bottles

These tall, narrow bottles are the classic baby bottle shape. Avoid using clear plastic (or glass) bottles to store breast milk.

European-style bottles

Shorter and wider than traditional bottles, these plastic bottles are particularly easy to clean. Some parents and babies also find their wide, rounded shape easier to grasp. Some brands offer handles, spouts, and straws that convert the bottles to training cups.

Angled bottles

Relative newcomers, these cylindrical bottles bend at a 45-degree angle at the top, which is supposed to prevent the baby from swallowing air. Some manufacturers also include a vent at the bottom that directs air away from the nipple.

Disposable bottles

Disposable nursers consist of a cylindrical plastic holder that holds a disposable plastic liner. The liners collapse as the baby feeds, minimizing the swallowing of air. Plastic liners are sterilized and one fewer thing to wash. Their drawbacks are expense, ecological concerns, and the fact that they cannot be heated in all bottle warmers.

Novelty bottles

Shaped like anything from animals to Coke bottles, novelty bottles are not designed for feeding infants. They rarely have ounce measurements on the sides and tend to be irregularly shaped and hard to hold.

Nipples

There are many different styles of nipples to choose from. Nipples come in latex and silicone. Silicone nipples are clear

Nipples

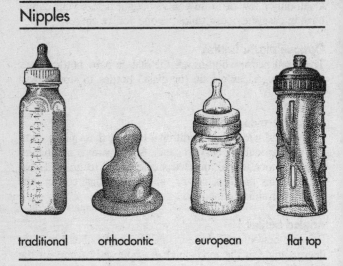

traditional   orthodontic   european   flat top

and taste- and odor-free and don't deteriorate as quickly as latex. They are also easier to clean and are dishwasher-safe. Latex nipples elongate in a baby's mouth while suckling, more closely approximating the shape of the human nipple during breast-feeding. Nipples also come with different size holes (preemie, newborn, infant, and toddler), which control the rate at which the contents of the bottle flow. Although most babies will accept any style of nipple offered to them from birth, some are more particular and may feed better with a different shape or flow rate, so you may want to experiment. Here are the most common nipple shapes.

Traditional
Short, with a narrow base and tip.

Orthodontic
Longer, with a wider base and flattened tip that is supposed to mimic the shape of the breast when the baby is suckling.

Orthodontic nipples must be positioned properly in the baby's mouth.

European

Shaped to fit the wider mouth of the bottles they come with, these silicone nipples have a very wide base and long tip.

Flat top

These nipples come with disposable bottles. They have a wide base and short, flat nipple which extends when the baby sucks. Orthodontic and round-tipped nipples are also available for use with disposable bottle holders.

Bottle-Feeding Accessories

There is an array of accessories available to help keep bottles and nipples clean and organized.

Steam sterilizer

Some pediatricians recommend sterilizing bottles and nipples until an infant is three months old. You can sterilize bottles and silicone nipples in the dishwasher or in a pot of boiling water. (Sterilizing latex in the dishwasher is not recommended because the detergent causes the latex to break down quickly.) But a steam sterilizer is safer and easier to use. Both electric and microwave steam sterilizers sterilize bottles, caps, and nipples in about 10 minutes without risk of overheating or splattering. If you won't be using a bottle immediately after sterilizing it, fill it right away and store it in the refrigerator.

Electric bottle warmer

This is a convenient alternative to heating bottles in hot water. Bottle warmers can be placed anywhere, including by the side of your bed for middle-of-the-night feedings. Some bottle warmers heat only traditional reusable bottles, while others heat any type of bottle, and even jars of baby food. The best feature to look for is a refrigerator compartment that keeps bottles cool until you are ready to warm them.

⚠️   **PARENTS ALERT**   ⚠️

Heating bottles in the microwave: Resist the temptation to heat bottles in the microwave. The liquid could heat unevenly, creating hot spots that could burn your baby. Microwaving may also destroy some of the nutrients in breast milk.

Bottle brush

This round brush with a long handle is a necessity for getting bottles thoroughly clean. Some have suction cups that secure them to your sink so they don't get lost.

Nipple brush

This tiny brush helps clean nipples. Turn nipples inside out for the most thorough cleaning.

Dishwasher basket

This small plastic basket keeps nipples, bottle rings, pacifiers, and teethers together in the dishwasher—and keeps them from flying all over during its operation.

Bottle drying rack

This rack has a series of wooden or plastic sticks from which you can hang bottles and nipples while they air dry.

Tongs

To handle sterilized bottles.

Long-handled spoon

For mixing formula. Get a plastic spoon that can be boiled or sterilized in the dishwasher.

Bottle organizer

There are many organizers with multiple compartments to
store bottles, nipples, and pacifiers in your cabinet or on
your countertop. Some have handles for easy portability.
Others incorporate a drying rack and dishwasher baskets.
Shop around for the one that best suits your needs.

Pacifiers

Although pacifiers are not technically feeding items, it
makes sense to discuss them in conjunction with bottle nipples. If you decide to give your baby a pacifier, make sure to
choose one that has no loose parts and has ventilation holes
in the shield (the Consumer Product Safety Commission requires this), which helps prevent any saliva that collects
around it from chapping your baby's lips or cheeks.

Like nipples, pacifiers come in latex and silicone, with
rounded or orthodontic shaped nipples. Silicone is less
likely to trigger an allergic reaction in sensitive babies than
latex. Keeping nipple and pacifier shape consistent is more
comfortable and less confusing for the baby.

If your baby is breast-feeding, it's best not to give her a
pacifier (or a bottle) for the first three to four weeks, or until
nursing is well established. Some babies develop "nipple
confusion" early on because the breast and the artificial nipple require different sucking actions.

Sterilize a pacifier before the first use, or if it falls into

---

⚠️ **PARENTS ALERT** ⚠️

Pacifier ribbons: Never attach a cord, string, or ribbon to
a pacifier. It could wrap around the baby's fingers or toes
and cut off circulation, or strangle the baby if it becomes
wrapped around her neck.

SHOULD YOU GIVE YOUR BABY A PACIFIER?

Pacifiers can be wonderfully soothing for babies—and parents—and aren't harmful if used judiciously. A recent study, however, does recommend limited pacifier use. It found a decreased incidence of ear infections in babies ages 7–18 months when their pacifier use was restricted to bedtime. The researchers speculate that frequent sucking on a pacifier could alter pressure in the middle ear and impair the functioning of the eustachian tubes. Any built-up fluid can then become infected by a bacteria or virus.

To avoid nipple confusion, breast-feeding newborns should not be given a pacifier for the first three to four weeks. Bottle-feeding newborns should be offered a pacifier only after it has been determined that they are not hungry; otherwise, the baby may satisfy her sucking need with the pacifier and refuse the bottle, leading to inadequate nutrition.

Pacifiers are especially useful during the second and third months, when sucking needs are greatest and few babies have the coordination to get their hands or fingers into their mouths. After three months, many parents discontinue pacifier use because they prefer to let their babies develop a self-soothing habit like thumb- or finger-sucking. These parents feel that self-soothing is preferable to pacifiers because the thumb or finger is always available and can't be lost in the middle of the night. Pacifier use, however, can be discontinued by the parent at any time, in contrast to thumb-sucking, which is controlled by the child.

Another option for pacifier use is to wean your baby from it at about six months, when the need for supplementary sucking greatly diminishes. Many children who stop using a pacifier at this age never develop other sucking habits.

One last argument against continuing the pacifier into toddlerhood has to do with language development. It

SHOULD YOU GIVE YOUR BABY A PACIFIER?
(continued)

is difficult to speak—and impossible to speak clearly—with a pacifier in your mouth. Most experts agree that it's a good idea to wean your baby from the pacifier around her first birthday (if not before), while her language skills are relatively undeveloped and her memory is still short.

something heavily germ-laden, like a dirty diaper. Wash it in soap and hot water before each use or if it falls on the ground.

If you do use a pacifier, it's a good idea to buy lots of them so that you'll always be able to find a clean one when your baby needs it.

Pacifier clips
If you want to keep your baby's pacifier from falling on the ground, use a pacifier clip sold for that purpose. Never attach a pacifier to a string or ribbon, which is a strangulation hazard.

Seats

High Chairs
Age: 4 months–3 years
A high chair is another place where your baby will spend a lot of time during the first three years of her life, so choose one that's comfortable for her as well as convenient for you. High chairs come in several different styles and with many different features, so it's wise to do some research before buying.

High chairs are also the cause of many injuries, but almost all of them are the result of improper use. The most basic tenet of high chair safety: Always strap your baby in. This may seem obvious, but thousands of children are hurt every year from falling or climbing out of their high chairs. To prevent tipping, choose a high chair with a wide, stable base and wheels that lock. Never place a baby in a high chair within arm's reach of a wall, table, or counter, since pushing against any surface can result in tipping the chair. For ease of entry and exit, look for a tray mechanism that can be operated with one hand. Make sure, however, that it can't pinch the baby's fingers.

Most high chairs today combine metal or plastic bases with padded vinyl seats. Although vinyl high chairs offer many more features, some parents still prefer traditional wooden high chairs for their tasteful and classic appearance. Be aware, however, that choosing a wooden chair means forgoing features like oversized trays, padded seats, wheeled bases, foldability, and height adjustment.

If you decide to go with a high-tech high chair, consider these features.

Adjustable height
Two height levels are all you really need: full height for use with the tray, and table-height for use as a youth chair later.

Wheels
Wheels are a must for moving the high chair around the kitchen (and the house) with ease. Look for sturdy, stable casters with locks or brakes.

Reclining seat
This is a useful feature if you want to have your baby sit at the table with you during meals before she starts eating solids. (Feeding solid foods is safe only if the baby is in a fully upright position.)

Comfortable, easy-to-clean seat
Look for generous padding with a minimum of food-trapping quilting or tufting. White high chairs match most decors, but are difficult to keep clean. Surprisingly, solid black or navy presents the same problem. A subdued print on smooth vinyl is best.

Large, easy-to-operate tray

The tray should have an easy-to-use, one-handed release and the ability to detach completely from the chair. It should also have a rim around the edges to prevent spills.

Adjustable footrest

This gives the high chair a more custom fit that may be more comfortable for your child as she grows.

Ability to fold

This is an important feature if you plan to travel with your high chair. It's also helpful when storing the chair. The folding mechanism should lock when the high chair is set up.

Sturdy, comfortable restraints

The restraining belt should fit around the baby's waist and between her legs—a five point restraining system with shoulder straps is even better. Some high chairs come with a plastic crotch bar to prevent the baby from slipping under the seat. This is fine for an infant but may make the seat uncomfortable for an older child.

Booster Seats
Age: 9 months–3 years

A booster seat is a child-sized seat that rests on a regular chair and elevates the child to the height of the table. Some booster seats also have trays, making them almost interchangeable with high chairs. Booster seats used to be strictly for toddlers who had outgrown high chairs, but now many manufacturers are offering boosters with features that allow infants as young as eight or nine months to use them. While it's possible to get such a booster seat and forgo a high chair entirely, we don't recommend it because booster seats are much less stable and less comfortable. And while they're wonderful for travel and for older children, they tend not to provide the support—and the tray space—that a baby under two years old needs.

Most booster seats are made of hard plastic, though there

are a few that are made from a dense foam. Look for a booster seat that has sturdy straps both on the bottom—to secure the seat to the chair—and in the seat—to restrain the child. (You may be able to use a seat without a safety belt for an older toddler who you know will not try to climb out or tip the chair.) Make sure that the seat has rubber feet on the bottom, both to keep it from slipping and to protect the chair underneath.

Use booster seats only at the table—never in a car or the tub. Make sure that the seat you are setting it on is larger than the booster, and never place any cushions between the booster seat and the chair. If your child is large and strong enough to upset the seat even when she is strapped in, do not use a booster.

If you plan to travel with your booster seat, you may want to consider one that folds flat. (Fisher-Price's fold-down booster seat even comes with room under the seat to pack food and its own backpack carrying case.) If you plan to use a booster seat to feed an infant, look for one with a removable tray. A problem to look out for: seats that include trays often have higher than usual sides for the tray to attach to. This may prevent the seat from fitting under the table when it is used without the tray.

There are also booster seats that recline for infant use. As with reclining high chairs, this is a largely unnecessary feature, since infants should not be fed solid food until they are able to sit upright with support.

Seat Harnesses
Age: 8 months–3 years

This booster seat alternative allows an infant to safely sit directly on an adult chair. It's a fabric harness that fits around the baby's abdomen and between her legs, and is secured in back of the chair with wide Velcro straps. A seat harness may be a good thing to keep in your diaper bag for feedings when a high chair or booster chair is not available.

Clip-On Seats
Age: 6 months–3 years

A clip-on seat is a plastic-, cloth-, or vinyl-covered seat with backrest attached to a metal frame that clips onto the edge of a table like a vise. A clip-on seat is appropriate from the time a baby can sit well unsupported until she is too tall or heavy for the seat (about 35 pounds). Clip-on seats are great if you want your baby to join the family at the table, and they're also wonderful for travel since they fold flat. When using one, be aware that the baby now has access to everything within reach on the table. Move things away judiciously and watch her closely to avoid accidents.

There are some limits to the usefulness of clip-on seats, since they can be safely attached only to certain types of tables. Never use a clip-on with a glass table, a pedestal table, a table that is even slightly unstable, or a tabletop that is thinner or thicker than specified in the clip-on chair's instructions.

Solid-Food Accessories

When your baby begins eating solid food, you enter a whole new world of mealtime adventures and the equipment they entail. Although all you really need during the baby-food stage is a soft-tipped spoon and a cereal bowl, there are many products available that will make preparing, serving, and storing your baby's food easier and more convenient.

Spoons and Forks
Infant feeding spoons

These spoons have a long handle and a small bowl, usually coated with vinyl so the baby can bite down on it comfortably. Stock up on four to six of these before you start your baby on solid food. Some spoons have a built-in temperature gauge and turn a different color if the food is too hot—but don't rely only on the spoon for this information. Infant spoons are not designed to be used by the baby—the long, straight handle makes them too unwieldy for little hands.

⚠ PARENTS ALERT ⚠

Lead in dishes: Make sure that any china or ceramic dishes you serve your child from do not have lead in their glaze. Ingesting lead can cause brain damage and other health problems, especially in children under six. Lead was used in many ceramic glazes until the 1980s and is still found in some imported dishes and pottery, especially those that are handmade or highly decorated. Heating in the microwave and use with acidic foods such as tomato sauce can cause greater quantities of lead to leach into food. Home lead testing kits are available at hardware stores and you can get additional information from the Environmental Protection Agency's National Lead Information Center (the NLIC's toll-free hotline is 800-532-3394). If you have any doubt about lead in your dishes, do not use them for your baby's food.

Toddler utensils
Toddler spoons and forks (no knives please) are miniature versions of flatware designed for self-feeding. Made of plastic, metal, or a combination of both, toddler utensils feature short handles and small (though not as tiny as infant-sized) bowls. Many toddler utensils have curved handles, which make it easier for the toddler to direct the food into her mouth. Some come with their own plastic cases for travel.

Bowls and Dishes
Forget that heirloom bone china with the nursery rhyme characters motif. Baby bowls should be unbreakable plastic that is dishwasher- and microwave-safe (there are plastics that are not). For spoon-feeding, a contoured bowl with a handle is very convenient. For self-feeding, nothing beats a suction-cup bottom. Many toddlers also appreciate divided plates, so that different foods don't touch each other—a not uncommon toddler pet peeve. Freezer- and microwave-safe bowls and dishes with airtight covers are great for both storing

SAFE FOOD STORAGE AND PREPARATION

Feeding your baby safely is easy if you follow these rules:

- Before opening baby food jars, rinse them under water or wipe with a damp cloth to remove dirt and dust.
- Make sure the button on the top of the baby food jar is down when you buy it and pops up when the jar is opened. If you don't hear the pop, don't use the food.
- When preparing homemade baby foods, make sure all utensils and work surfaces that come in contact with the food are clean.
- Wash all fruits and vegetables in detergent and water and rinse well. Better yet, peel them.
- Never mix raw egg with your baby's food. It can harbor salmonella.
- If you heat baby food in the microwave, let it sit for a minute after heating and then stir well to avoid hot spots. Taste it or test some on your inner wrist before serving.
- If you taste your baby's food, wash the spoon or use a fresh one for her.
- Don't feed the baby directly from the jar unless you plan to use it all, because saliva from the spoon begins to digest the food and causes it to spoil more quickly. For the same reason, don't save a bowl of food your baby has already been fed from.
- Don't use opened baby food that has been at room temperature for longer than an hour.
- If you're feeding an older baby canned foods, make sure your can opener is clean. Never feed your baby food from cans that are swollen, dented, or leaky.
- Refrigerate baby food after opening. Fruits and juices can be stored in the refrigerator for three days; everything else, for two days. After that, throw it away.

SAFE FOOD STORAGE AND PREPARATION
(continued)

- If you need to transport previously opened jars of baby food, keep them cool with an ice pack in an insulated bag. Do not use it if the food no longer feels cool.
- When it doubt, throw it out.

---

food and traveling. Small snack cups with lids are also handy once you start carrying Cheerios and banana slices everywhere you go.

Training Cups
Age: 6 months–3 years

Widely known as Sippy cups, these covered and spouted plastic cups provide a transition from drinking from a bottle to drinking from a cup. Training cups are available in many different styles, and users are often fiercely loyal to the one they favor. Take the following features and your baby's preferences into consideration when choosing a Sippy cup.

Handles
One or two handles allow beginning drinkers to grasp the cup more easily.

Rounded or weighted bottom
This helps keep the cup upright.

Soft-spout lid
The soft spout is more like a nipple, so it is easiest for young babies. However, it spills easily when tipped.

Fold-down spout
Snaps closed for travel.

Spill-proof spout

These cups are almost completely spill-proof—liquid will not splatter if the baby turns the cup upside down and shakes it or waves it around. For easier cleaning, choose a cup with a membrane—a thin, flexible piece of plastic with a slit in it that allows air to escape when the baby sucks on the spout—rather than a separate valve. The downside to spill-proof cups is that the baby has to work harder to get the liquid out, which may frustrate a beginning sipper.

Screw-on top

A screw-on top is harder for the baby to remove than a snap-on lid.

Straw top

Some babies find it easier to sip from a straw than a spout. Look for a short straw that folds down for travel and removes easily for cleaning.

Sports bottle

Babies suck on these pop-up bottles rather than squirting them into their mouths. Some prefer a sports bottle to a cup, although neither sports bottles nor straws help teach cup-drinking skills.

Contoured shape

Some Sippy cups have a modified hourglass shape for easier gripping.

Bibs
Age: Birth–3 years

From tiny drool bibs for newborns to smocklike coverups for toddlers, there's a bib suitable for every age and stage. And once your baby starts eating solids, you can never have too many. Choose bibs with Velcro or snap fasteners, or a ribbed neck that slips over the head. String ties are difficult to fasten onto a squirming baby and can pose a strangulation hazard.

Drool bib

These little cloth bibs are designed for infants to wear to protect their clothes from drool and spit-up. Made of soft, absorbent terry cloth or flannel, they usually feature appliqués, characters, or sayings such as "Spit happens." Buy two or three for your layette—you can always add more later if your baby drools or spits up a lot.

Chin bib

Tinier even than drool bibs, these narrow fabric bibs protect the area under the baby's chin from rash and are especially useful when she is teething. These are for drool only; they're too small to protect against spit-up or food.

Feeding bib

These are the workhorses of the bib wardrobe—you'll need at least eight once your baby starts solids. Feeding bibs protect a baby's clothes from the messy ordeal of mealtime. Standard feeding bibs fasten around the neck and cover the front of the shirt. Some have a pocket at the bottom to catch spills. Feeding bibs come in many fabrics, all of which can be machine washed and dried; the exception are plastic bibs, which can be wiped down with a paper towel or sponge. Some bibs have novelty features like attached toys or teething edges, which seem to defeat the purpose of protecting clothes from mess, as the baby is sure to want to lift them up and explore.

Feeding bibs come in several materials:

- *Cotton.* Cotton (usually terry cloth) is pliable, absorbent, and washes well, but it tends to stain. Some cotton bibs are backed with vinyl to make them waterproof. Some parents prefer cotton bibs because they feel softest against a baby's neck.
- *Vinyl.* Vinyl bibs are stain resistant and clean up easily, but they may feel heavy or sticky around a baby's neck and may crack with age. Look for vinyl backed with fabric to minimize discomfort.

- *Nylon.* A wonderful fabric for bibs, nylon is light-weight and pliable, washes or wipes clean easily, and dries almost instantly. It is also waterproof, so liquids won't soak through.
- *Plastic.* Molded plastic bibs offer the ultimate protection against wetness and wipe clean easily. On the downside, plastic is heavy for tiny necks and can be sticky and uncomfortable.

Coverall bib
Meant for bigger kids who make bigger messes, these bibs feature short or long sleeves to protect shoulders and arms. Coverall bibs come in fabric, nylon, and vinyl.

Disposable bib
These paper bibs with plastic backing are handy for dining out. Most disposables have adhesive tape that sticks directly to the baby's clothes. Great for wiping faces, too, disposable bibs usually come in packs of 20 to 30. They don't offer maximum protection, but it's often worth it not to have to bring a messy bib home in your bag.

Feeding Accessories
Safe feeder
This is a little mesh bag attached to a plastic handle. A piece of soft fresh fruit or vegetable is placed in the bag, and the baby is supposed to be able to chew on the food without the risk of choking. True, this product does prevent choking, but it pretty much prevents eating as well. Most babies enjoy their food a lot less when they have to chew it out of a fabric bag. Cutting the food into tiny pieces and supervising your baby while she eats is a much better alternative.

Splat mat
Just what it sounds like. This is a large, square sheet of vinyl that is placed under the high chair (or wherever the baby is eating) to protect the floor. Some parents find this very con-

RESTAURANT CHECKLIST

Dining out with your baby starts easy and gets progressively more difficult. The one-year-old year—when food flies and baby spends the meal screeching to get out of her high chair—is probably the most difficult. Like anything else, eating out with a baby or toddler is a lot more likely to be pleasant if you come prepared. From the age of 2 months, many babies are fascinated by ceiling fans and neon lights, so a diner can be a good choice. Avoid very noisy—or very quiet—restaurants. Here's what to bring:

Birth–6 months
- Carrier-style infant car seat
- Diaper bag stocked with diapers and wipes
- Bottle of formula or breast milk (if you give your baby bottles)
- Nursing shawl or receiving blanket (if you are breast-feeding)
- Burp cloths or cloth diapers
- Toy or toy bar to hang from the carrier handle

6–12 months
- Clip-on seat or booster seat with tray if there are no high chairs available (a sign that the restaurant is not very child friendly)
- Diaper bag stocked with diapers and wipes
- Extra outfit
- Bottle of formula or breast milk (if you give your baby bottles)
- Nursing shawl or receiving blanket (if you are breast-feeding)
- One or two jars of baby food (even if your baby is eating finger foods, since there might not be anything appropriate on the menu)
- Bib

RESTAURANT CHECKLIST

- Feeding spoon
- Dry finger foods like Cheerios or thin, unsalted pretzels broken into tiny pieces
- Disposable placemat if your baby is eating finger foods
- Small toys or teethers (you may want to hook them onto the baby's seat with plastic links)

12–18 months
- Clip-on seat or booster seat with tray if needed
- Diaper bag stocked with diapers and wipes
- Extra outfit
- Bottle or Sippy cup
- Baby food, if your baby still eats it, and feeding spoon
- Bib
- Toddler spoon
- Dry finger foods
- Disposable placemat
- Small toys or books

18 months–3 years
- Clip-on seat or booster seat if needed
- Diaper bag stocked with diapers and wipes
- Extra outfit (including underwear if your child is toilet-taught)
- Sippy cup
- Bib
- Toddler utensils
- Crackers or other dry snacks
- Small toys or books
- Crayons and paper or coloring book

venient; others think it's easier to clean the floor than to clean and dry the mat. This is a must-have for feeding a baby in a carpeted room.

Placemat

A placemat is not appropriate until your toddler reaches the age where she will not immediately fling it—and all that's on it—to the floor. Once your child is old enough, she will enjoy using a vinyl placemat with a bright design on it. This is a good opportunity to introduce concepts like colors, shapes, animals, and letters in a fun, low-pressure setting. Disposable placemats are great for eating out. These thin plastic mats have adhesive strips that secure them to the table and protect your baby and the table from each other.

Food Preparation Equipment

Food mill

If you plan to make your own baby food, a hand-operated food grinder is indispensable. Compact, portable, inexpensive, and easy to clean, this little gadget does what a food processor often cannot—turn fresh foods into strained baby food that's just the right consistency for an infant. Baby food mills are cylindrical in shape with a handle or cap to turn the blades and grind fruits, vegetables, or meats. Some come with a carrying case, feeding dish, or feeding spoon. They also come with a booklet that explains how to safely prepare baby foods.

Formula pitcher

Marketed as special formula-mixing systems, these are simply plastic pitchers with measurement marks on the side and a built-in mixing stick. Any plastic pitcher and spatula will do the job just as well.

Formula mixing bottle

This is a feeding bottle that is specially made to store powdered formula and water separately until you are ready to use them. The bottle is filled with eight ounces of water and formula measured into an internal chamber. When you're ready to use it, just twist the top and shake. This is a great invention for travel or for middle-of-the-night formula feedings.

Chapter 4

Travel

The minute you bring your baby home, your days of running out of the house with nothing but your wallet and keys are over. From now on (for the next two or three years, anyway), you'll be toting diapers, wipes, bottles, snacks, toys, and changes of clothes everywhere you go. You'll need a car seat for every automobile ride your baby takes and a stroller or baby carrier if you want to take a walk. All this may sound overwhelming, but you'll be surprised how quickly you'll get used to traveling with this gear and how soon you'll become proficient in knowing just what you need to get you where you're going. Make wise choices when selecting travel gear, because having the right things will make your life infinitely easier—the rest is just extra baggage.

Diaper Bags

Age: Birth–3 years

There's no such thing as traveling light with a baby, so you'll need a trusty diaper bag to carry all the gear. Diaper bags come in a myriad of styles, shapes, and sizes. When you're considering your options, keep in mind that this bag will probably replace your pocketbook for the next two years or so. Although nursery rhyme prints or pastels may look cute on the store shelf, try to imagine what they will look like hanging from your—or your spouse's—shoulder. In the long run, you'll probably be happiest with a solid, neutral-colored bag.

Diaper bags come in two basic styles, tote and backpack. Within these categories you'll find many different sizes, shapes, and features. Tote-style bags sling over the shoulder (some also have handles for briefcase-style carrying) and open on top. They may be shaped like large pocketbooks, small suitcases, or "schoolbags," with a big flap in the front. Some have a sporty look, others have a high-fashion style, and still others have a more traditional juvenile look. Tote-style diaper bags are usually spacious and often include many compartments and features. They are especially practical for long trips and for parents toting equipment for more than one child.

Backpack-style diaper bags are usually smaller than totes and may have a sporty or high-fashion look. Though they look like regular backpacks, they usually have an insulated compartment for bottles, a changing pad, and other baby-friendly features. They are comfortable and convenient to carry, and often pack a lot of features into a compact space. The downside of some backpacks is that they have only one top-loading main compartment without any dividers. This tends to make for jumbled, disorganized contents and difficult access to the things on the bottom. Some backpacks solve this problem with a special zipper that provides access to the bottom of the pack without having to

PACKING THE PERFECT DIAPER BAG

Restock your diaper bag right after you return from an outing rather than right before you leave. This will save lots of last-minute rushing around and prevent you from **ever** being caught without an extra diaper or a change **of** clothes. Here are the necessities for everyday outings; adjust accordingly for longer trips:

- Three to six diapers (depending upon the age of your baby—younger babies will need more than older ones). Always pack one more diaper than you think you'll need.
- Travel-size pack of baby wipes. You can also carry wipes in a zip-top plastic bag.
- Small container or tube of diaper cream.
- Changing pad.
- Large zip-top plastic bag (as a backup to the waterproof pouch that comes with the diaper bag).
- Change of clothes for your baby.
- Cloth diapers or a small towel for protecting your shoulder against spit-up.
- Pacifier (if your baby uses one) in a plastic bag.
- Extra receiving blanket or sweater.
- Small toys, books, or teethers.
- Unopened jar of baby food and a spoon in a plastic bag for a younger baby; healthy dry snacks like Cheerios, graham crackers, or salt-free pretzels for an older baby or toddler.
- Bib—preferably one that wipes clean or is disposable.
- Sunscreen (all year round). Use a PABA-free formula with an SPF of 15 or higher that is especially formulated for babies.
- Sun hat (in summer).
- Bottle of formula or Sippy cup of juice or water. These, of course, cannot be packed in advance.

open the top. If the backpack has only one main compartment, make sure it also has a front pouch for your wallet and keys.

Whichever style of diaper bag you choose, it should be durable and practical as well as good-looking.

Here's what's important:
- Tough, rip-resistant, easy-to-clean fabric. Look for densely woven nylon or polyester rather than vinyl or quilted cotton.
- Waterproof interior, for obvious reasons.
- Wide padded straps on backpack styles.
- Several compartments, or one main compartment with mesh dividers or zippered pockets.
- Separate compartment for parents' things.
- Large, lightweight, waterproof changing pad.
- Waterproof pouch for wet things.
- Outside bottle pockets with elastic top or easily accessible bottle compartment. An insulated pocket is a nice bonus. Avoid bags with only elastic straps inside to hold bottles—the bottles won't stay upright, and their moisture will dampen the other contents of the bag.

Mini diaper bags
If you don't want to lug your entire diaper bag with you when you run out to do a quick errand, a mini diaper bag is handy for carrying a couple of diapers, some wipes, a bottle, and your wallet and keys. Mini diaper bags come in shoulder and hip (fanny-pack) styles; several convert to both. These probably won't come with a changing pad, but look for a durable fabric, a waterproof interior, and a separate bottle pocket.

Strollers

Age: Birth–3 years

As you set out to choose a stroller, the best way to make an informed decision is to read up on features and options, and then go test drive the strollers yourself. If you plan to buy a stroller from a catalogue or online, try to find and try the same model before you buy.

No matter which style of stroller you buy, you should consider the following features:

- *Handle height.* Many stroller handles are uncomfortably low. Everyone who will be using the stroller regularly should be comfortable with the handle height. Some models have telescoping handles; others can be used with handle extenders.

- *Weight.* The lighter the stroller, the easier it is to get in and out of the car. The heavier the stroller, the more solid it will feel.

- *Ease of folding.* Fold and unfold several times any stroller you are considering buying and make sure you are comfortable using the mechanism. One-handed folding is best. Make sure the stroller folds down compact enough to fit comfortably in the trunk of your car or wherever you plan to store it.

- *Seat position.* If you'll be using the stroller for a newborn, the seat must recline fully. Look for an easy-to-use, one-handed reclining mechanism.

- *Wheels.* Look for wheels that provide some traction. Bigger wheels generally give a smoother ride. Wheels should swivel smoothly when turned and lock securely.

- *Fabric.* Best is a stroller cover that is removable for easy washing. Next best is fabric that can be wiped down with a damp cloth. Dark fabric hides stains better than light. Avoid gender-specific fabrics unless you don't plan to use the stroller for another child.

- *Canopy.* Any stroller you plan to use outdoors should have a full sun canopy. A flat shade will not provide enough protection. Look for a canopy with a window on top so you can see your baby.
- *Basket.* A deep, roomy basket beneath the seat with easy access is a must if you're going to take your stroller on shopping trips. Don't let anyone convince you that a mesh stroller bag is a good substitute for a basket.

There are also several safety features you should be aware of:
- *Safety straps.* Make sure the restraining straps lock securely and include a strap that goes between the legs. A five-point harness, with shoulder straps, is even safer for older babies and toddlers. *Always strap your baby in.* Never leave even a newborn unstrapped: the baby could wriggle down and fall out the end of the stroller.
- *Latches.* Make sure all latches lock firmly in place when the stroller is set up.
- *Enclosed headrest.* The area where the baby's head rests in a reclining stroller should have raised sides to keep the baby's head and arms from becoming caught in the frame.

There are also less essential features that are available on some stroller models. Here's the lowdown on the bells and whistles:
- *Snack tray.* Toddlers may enjoy the novelty of a tray with a cupholder, but it gets in the way if you're using the stroller for an infant. Some snack trays are detachable.
- *Handle tray and cup holder.* Can be handy, but not worth the extra weight it adds. Get a clip-on cup holder instead.
- *All-terrain wheels.* These large rubber wheels are great if you plan to push your stroller over grass, sand,

or dirt. They're overkill if the roughest terrain you'll encounter is cracked linoleum at the mall.

- **Reversible handle.** This lets you push the stroller with the baby facing either toward or away from you. It's a great feature if you're going to be using the stroller from birth through toddlerhood.
- **Rocker.** Some strollers have a mechanism that allows the chassis to rock back and forth. The motion of the stroller itself, however, is enough to calm most babies.
- **Boot.** This fabric sleeve fits over the end of the stroller and encloses the baby's feet. It may add some protection from cold weather, but an extra blanket can serve the same purpose. The boot is not a restraining device and should never be used in place of safety straps.

Carriages and Convertible Carriage/Strollers
Age: Birth and up

Your baby's first carriage must allow him to lie down in a flat position. This is only necessary for the first three months or so (after which most babies can be comfortably propped in a semi-reclining position), so a pram or baby carriage that does not convert into a stroller is either a luxury or a waste of money, depending on your perspective.

Many companies make carriages that convert to strollers. Their seat positions range from flat to upright, and their handles can usually be reversed, so you can push your baby facing you as you would with a true carriage. Many convertible strollers also have full hoods and a boot to provide infants with more protection from the elements. Their downside is that they tend to be heavy and cumbersome to fold. Many families invest in a convertible to use for walks around the neighborhood and add a lightweight stroller to keep in the car once the baby can sit up.

Infant Car Seat/ Stroller Systems
Age: Birth and up

This handy system consists of a carrier-style infant car seat that attaches to a mid-sized stroller. The carrier is used in the car with a base as a rear-facing infant car seat, and then lifted out and attached to the stroller. This wonderful invention allows you to move a sleeping baby from car to stroller without disturbing him. When the baby is old enough to sit in a forward-facing stroller, the base stroller is used without the car seat.

This is a versatile and economical product, as long as the stroller that comes with it is one that you are happy to use. The strollers do tend to be on the large and heavy side, and do not fold down small enough to store in a tight space like the overhead compartment on a plane.

Lightweight Strollers
Age: Birth and up

Lightweight strollers come in many shapes and sizes, and range in weight up to about 15 pounds. Some recline completely and are appropriate for a baby from birth; others have only one, upright position and can be used from the time a baby can sit unaided—usually at six to seven months. Lightweight strollers are available with a range of features similar to regular strollers. They are the most convenient for traveling, whether to the local mall or across the country. Their only drawbacks are that you can't use many of them for newborns and some seats on these strollers aren't roomy enough for large toddlers or preschoolers. High-quality lightweight strollers are often the stroller of choice for city dwellers.

Umbrella Strollers
Age: 6 months and up

Umbrella strollers, so named because they can be folded up and hung over your arm from their hooked handles like an umbrella, are simple and economical. They consist of fabric slung from a metal frame, and are low-priced, portable, and fold down to a very small size. The downside of umbrellas is their lack of features. These strollers do not recline, so they may not be used until your baby can sit independently. The wheels are usually small and there are no baskets or sun canopies (though some have sun shades). An umbrella stroller is ideal as a backup or a travel stroller.

Jogging Strollers
Age: 6 months and up

These strollers feature bicycle wheels and sleek aluminum frames. The tires are wonderful for rough terrain like grass and sand, and they glide smoothly over roads at speeds of up to 15 miles per hour. Some of the newest crop of jogging strollers feature reclining seats (but are still not appropriate for babies who cannot yet support their own heads) and fold down to fit in a large car trunk. Look for a model with a hand brake and tether strap so the stroller can't get away from you if you accidentally let go while you're running. Choose 20-inch wheels if you really run; 12- or 16-inch wheels are fine for jogging or walking at a fast clip. Jogging strollers also come in double and triple models, and in single and double models that convert to a bike trailer.

Double Strollers
Age: Birth and up

You'll need a double stroller if your family includes twins or both an infant and a toddler. The double stroller market has blossomed recently, and now includes strollers in every category, from umbrella to all-terrain jogging. There are two basic types of double stroller: front-and-back and side-by-side.

Front-and-back stroller

These are the width of a single stroller and have two (or more—up to five) in-line seats. The back seat usually reclines fully, the front only partially, making this a practical choice for a newborn and older child, as it allows the older child a good view from the front seat and the infant to sleep undisturbed in the back. These strollers are usually heavy (although lighter-weight aluminum ones are available at higher prices) and well padded. Most include a spacious basket, and sun canopies for each child. They have the advantage of being narrow and therefore relatively easy to maneuver in tight spaces, but they may not fold as easily or compactly as their side-by-side counterparts. A few front-and-back models allow you to flip the seats so the children can face each other. This option also often allows you to fully recline both seats.

Side-by-side stroller

These look like two (or three) strollers standing next to each other. They come in simple umbrella styles and larger models packed with extra features. Look for independently reclining seats (many recline fully) and two separate or one double sun canopy. These strollers come in large, sturdy models that fold flat (making them a rather large item to store) or smaller, umbrella models that fold down to a size that's not much bigger than a single umbrella stroller. Most of these these models, however, do not have baskets). Such a stroller will take multiples from birth through toddlerhood. Their only drawback is that their girth usually makes them unwieldy on narrow sidewalks or in mazelike stores, though a few companies offer a model that's only 30 inches (or less) in width.

Sit-and-stand stroller

These are for families with an infant and an older toddler or preschooler and consist of one regular stroller seat with a platform and simple jump seat behind it. One model accommodates an infant car seat in place of the stroller seat; another accommodates three children (two seats and one jump seat).

When the older child wants to ride on the stroller, he can stand on the platform or sit (facing backward) on the jump seat. There is a safety belt for both positions. Sit-and-stand strollers are smaller, lighter, and easier to fold than traditional back-and-front doubles and are useful for an older child who needs the stroller only for an occasional rest. This is not a particularly comfortable ride, though, so if your three- or four-year-old will be a frequent passenger, opt for a traditional double stroller.

Stroller Bases
Age: Birth–9 months
This is an ingenious device that turns an infant car seat into a stroller. Major car seat brands secure onto this stroller base, but unlike the car seat/stroller system, this base does not become a stroller in its own right after your baby grows out of the infant car seat (at 20 pounds). It is, however, much lighter and easier to fold, and the deluxe model has a large storage basket. This is an excellent product for someone who wants the convenience of a car seat stroller without the weight or the commitment to a certain stroller.

Car Seat Strollers
Age: Birth and up
It's a bird, it's a plane, it's a car seat that converts to a stroller and a booster seat! The ultimate in versatility, this car seat can be used rear-facing for infants and front-facing for toddlers. Pop out the wheels and the handle, and it's a stroller. Retract both, and it can be used as a booster seat at the table. The problem with all this versatility is that while this product does a lot of jobs, it does none of them particularly well. It's a cumbersome car seat; a heavy, low-to-the-ground stroller; and a large, unstable booster seat. You are much better off with a stroller/car seat system. The only exception: If you often travel by air, this seat goes from car to airport to plane and back again without any additional pieces to tote and track.

WHICH STROLLER IS RIGHT FOR YOU?

There are so many different kinds of strollers on the market today that it can be overwhelming for a first-time parent to sort through all the options. The best stroller for you might not be the one that's right for your neighbor or best friend. Where you live, the age of your baby, the number of children in your family, and the places you go are all important and individual factors that go into making a decision about which stroller—or strollers—to buy.

For the first four or five months of your baby's life, you'll need a stroller or pram that allows him to lie flat. If you live in the suburbs and travel mostly by car, a stroller/car seat system or a stroller that allows you to attach an infant car seat may be your best bet. Another option is to get a stroller base to use for the first months and then a good-quality lightweight stroller when your baby can sit up. Other parents may prefer to buy a convertible stroller to use for walks around the neighborhood and long day trips plus a lightweight or umbrella stroller to leave in the car.

If you live in a city and walk almost everywhere, or if you plan to use your stroller as a bassinet, a sturdy, comfortable convertible stroller that reclines fully is a practical choice. You may also want to purchase a small lightweight or umbrella stroller for times when you need to take public transportation.

If your lifestyle includes running with your baby or a lot of strolling off the pavement (on the grass in the park, down a gravel driveway, at the beach), a jogging stroller is an excellent investment. High-end ultralight models are for serious runners. A jogger with 12- or 16-inch wheels and a sturdier frame (and lower price) are fine for joggers, walkers, and parkgoers.

A final point of consideration is whether, and when,

WHICH STROLLER IS RIGHT FOR YOU?
(continued)

you plan to have more children. If you plan to add a second with in a year or two after the birth of your first, you'll soon be in the market for a double stroller. If you're shopping for your final child, on the other hand, be sure to take into account whether he will be able to fit into the stroller you choose when he's a strapping preschooler.

Stroller Accessories
Age: Birth and up
Mosquito netting
Covers the stroller to protect your baby from bugs. Comes in single- or double-stroller sizes.

Weather shield
This plastic shield covers the stroller to protect your baby from wind, rain, and snow. Look for one with mesh windows on the side for ventilation. A must for the urban baby.

UV-blocking mesh
This mesh shield attaches to the stroller canopy and blocks out 97 percent of ultraviolet rays. It also serves as a wind, rain, and insect shield. This is something to consider if your baby will be strolling in the sun for long periods of time.

Insect repeller
This battery-operated device clips onto the side of the stroller and emits a low hum that is supposed to mimic the sound of a dragonfly, a natural enemy of mosquitoes. If you really want to keep mosquitoes away from your baby, though, use netting.

⚠️ **PARENTS ALERT** ⚠️

Stroller safety: Many injuries occur through misuse. Always strap your child securely in the stroller, and never leave him unattended in it—he could wriggle down and get his head caught in a leg opening. Make sure your stroller has a locking device to prevent accidental folding and brakes on at least two wheels. Use caution if you hang bags from the handle, which can cause the stroller to tip over. Look for JPMA certification to make sure your stroller meets the highest safety standards.

Stroller bunting

This quilted cover (nylon outside, polar fleece inside) zips around the seat and sides of the stroller and the baby so only his head is exposed. For older babies, the comforter can be zipped under the arms for more freedom of movement. This is a luxurious accessory for the city baby in winter.

Stroller fleece

This lambskin pad lines the stroller seat with fluffy wool. Looks comfortable, but it's a pain to clean and hinders stroller folding. Some babies may be allergic to wool.

Stroller fan

This small, battery-operated fan clips onto the stroller and blows a gentle breeze. Some babies like the feeling of wind on their faces, others do not.

Handle extenders

These add three to six inches to standard umbrella stroller handles.

Tote bag

This heavy-duty nylon bag encloses the folded stroller for protection when traveling.

Stroller toys

Some clip onto the frame; others attach to a bar or a snack tray that attaches to the front crossbar. To keep your baby from becoming bored, look for toy bars that can be re-arranged or that you can attach different toys to. It can't hurt to bring a few toys along, but the passing scenery is often enough to keep a baby interested.

Snack trays

These plastic trays attach to the front crossbar or the side of the stroller and hold snacks and a bottle or cup. They are handy for toddlers, who are less likely than infants to leave most of the food in a trail behind them.

Wheel weights

Stroller weights wrap around the front wheels of the stroller to help prevent tipping if you hang heavy bags from the back.

Drink/accessory holders

These plastic cups and hooks clip onto the handle or the side of the stroller to provide the parent with a place to store a drink or hang shopping bags. This is a useful accessory, especially when combined with wheel weights.

Stroller bag

If your stroller's basket is small or nonexistent, a stroller bag provides needed storage space. Traditional bags are made of mesh and hang from the back of the stroller frame. Updated versions consist of a nylon backing and different size storage pockets to aid in organization. Wheel weights are recommended to counter the loaded bag's weight.

Stroller connecters

These plastic clips join two umbrella strollers to make them into a double stroller. Fine in a pinch, but the connected strollers are hard to maneuver and easy to tip.

Stroller safety kit

This triangular case attaches to the side of the stroller and contains a reflective vest and basic first aid supplies like antiseptic wipes, bandages, and tweezers. The case itself is reflective, and a flashlight is strapped to the bottom. This is useful for strolling at night or if you just want to be extra safe.

Baby Carriers

Baby carriers allow you to carry your baby close to your body while freeing up your hands. Some parents swear by them, while others find them uncomfortable and impractical. There are several different types of carriers. Look for one that suits your baby's stage of development as well as your size and strength. You may want to try a few on friends' babies before buying, or at least keep the receipt in case you or your baby dislikes the one you buy.

Soft Front and Back Carriers
Age: Birth–10 months

Soft carriers are like little pouches with leg and arm holes that strap to your body and hold your baby against you, in front (facing your chest for newborns or facing out for older babies) or in back. Many newborns love to ride in front packs, probably because they find both your proximity and

---

 PARENTS ALERT

Baby carrier safety: Never, ever use a baby carrier in place of a car seat or when you are running, skating, or biking. Never cook while your baby is in a front pack, because hot food could splatter on him. Always bend at the knees when you're wearing a carrier to prevent your baby from falling out, and never climb a ladder or reach for an object overhead—it could fall on the baby.

the motion of your walking soothing. Some parents carry their babies in a front pack all day, letting the baby nap and even nurse right in the carrier.

For your own comfort, look for a soft carrier with thickly padded straps and a waist belt that adjusts to several different positions. For your baby's comfort and safety, look for soft, washable fabrics and secure snaps, buckles, and belts. If you're going to be carrying a newborn (facing inward only), make sure the carrier has a stiff back to support his head. Some headrests are made to fold down when the baby is older. If you're going to be using the carrier mainly around the house, choose one in a soft, lightweight cotton. If you plan to travel with the carrier, a sturdy nylon model with pockets for pacifiers and toys is best.

Side Carriers
Age: 6–18 months
Side carriers allow an older baby to ride strapped to your hip. Many mothers of heavier children find the hip carrier much more comfortable than a front carrier. Look for a sturdy side carrier with strong, padded, adjustable straps and a seat big enough for your baby to sit comfortably. Some front carriers convert to hip carriers. Make sure your baby can sit unassisted before using a side carrier with him.

Slings
Age: Birth–2 years
A baby sling is a soft, versatile front carrier that can be used for both infants and toddlers. A large, unconstructed piece of fabric that is gathered at both ends, the sling wraps around your chest and back and secures with an adjustable buckle at the shoulder. A newborn is carried in the "hammock" position, which allows him to lie in the sling with the fabric wrapped around him, holding him close to your chest. Many newborns find this position extremely soothing, because of the closeness to you, the swaying motion when you move, and the swaddling effect of the fabric. A sling is also excellent for discreet nursing.

As your baby gets older, he can be positioned to face out from your chest or to sit straddling your hip. Some experienced users even use the sling to carry their babies on their backs. Although the sling is extremely versatile, it does take some practice to use it confidently. Because there are no restraining straps, the baby must be positioned just right, so that he will stay in securely without being held by you. It may take a good deal of practice to get it right.

Look for a sling with plenty of padding at the shoulder and an adjustable two-ring buckle. Some higher-priced slings are available in petite and extra-large sizes. These are definitely worth the money if their size fits you better than the standard ones and you plan to use the sling regularly.

Framed Back Carriers
Age: 6 months–3 years
A framed back carrier is a fabric seat suspended from a metal or plastic frame. The frame sits against the wearer's back and distributes the weight of the child evenly so that there is less strain on the shoulders and back. The baby faces the wearer's back, and his legs and arms dangle. To ride safely in a back carrier, a baby must have full head and neck control and be able to sit unsupported. Babies usually reach these milestones between six and eight months. A framed backpack is wonderful for families that like to hike and walk in areas where it would be inconvenient or impossible to push a stroller. Most babies love riding in a backpack because it keeps them close to their parent and gives them a high vantage point from which to see the world.

When choosing a framed backpack, look for a light, ergonomic frame that adjusts to fit adults of different heights. It should have a well-padded waist strap and adjustable sternum straps and lumbar support panels. The seat and straps should be adjustable, and the pack should have a five-point restraint system for the baby. Nice extras are a removable, washable seat and storage pouches, bottle pockets, and toy loops. There is even a framed back pack that converts to a stroller. It's always wise to try before you buy, since a frame that's too heavy or bulky will be uncomfortable.

Twin and Triplet Carriers

Double and triple soft carriers are available for hale and hearty parents of multiples. In places where a stroller is impractical or a double stroller unwieldy, you might want to consider a single front carrier and a single stroller—or, in the supermarket, place one baby in a single front carrier and the other in the seat of the shopping cart.

Bicycle Child Seats
Age: 12 months and up

Bicycle child seats attach to your bicycle in back or in front of you so your toddler or preschooler can ride along with you. The seat is molded plastic, usually with a pad for comfort. Look for a seat that is sturdy and impact resistant, and that easily attaches and detaches from the bike. The seat should have a five-point restraining harness, a high backrest, and adjustable footrests. When your child is riding in a bike seat, he must wear a helmet that meets Consumer Product Safety Commission (CPSC) guidelines. Look for a helmet made especially for toddlers, with easy-to-adjust straps and adequate ventilation. Bike seats should not be used with children over 40 pounds. Exercise special care when mounting and dismounting, as the extra weight increases the risk of tipping over.

Car Seats

It's not only common sense—it's the law. Your child must sit in an approved car seat every time he rides in the car, from his trip home from the hospital until he is four years old or weighs 40 pounds (whichever comes second). It's unsafe (and illegal) to carry your baby in your lap, in a portable bassinet, or in an infant seat even for the shortest trip.

Resist the temptation to save money by buying a second-hand car seat. The model may not meet current safety standards or may have been recalled. It may have been in an accident and have unseen structural damage.

If your baby is born prematurely and you haven't had a chance to buy a car seat, inquire whether your hospital loans them out—many do. Your insurance company or local police department may also have a loan program or sell a certain model of car seat at a wholesale price. Also be aware that not every model of car seat fits well in every car. Try installing your car seat as soon as you buy it—if it doesn't fit, return it and try another one. Most police departments have an auto safety expert who can tell you which type of car seat is best for your car. Finally, it's a good idea to check *Consumer Reports* before you buy a car seat to find out the safety ratings on the most current models.

No matter which car seat you select, look for a removable, washable cover. There are three basic types of car seats—rear-facing infant, convertible, and booster—each with unique features.

As of September 2002, new cars and safety seats are required to come equipped with a standardized attachment system called Lower Anchors and Tethers for Children (LATCH), which makes installation much easier. Seats come with three attachment hooks—two at the bottom and one at the top—and cars have corresponding anchors. The location and design of the anchors vary greatly, so make sure you latch the seat to the proper anchor. Furthermore, be wary of using the center back seat, as car manufacturers are required to provide only two LATCH locations—and it's usually the two outside seats. (This can be confusing to parents who may have heard that the middle back seat is the safest place.) Finally, most recently designed forward-facing seats come with a tether strap, even if they don't have lower anchor attachments, and most vehicles since 1989 have built-in locations for anchors. If you have a car with no tether anchor, contact your dealership and have one installed, and use the tether strap.

Infant Car Seats
Age: Birth–12 months

Rear-facing infant car seats are specially designed for babies from birth to approximately 20 to 22 pounds (though some convertible car seats can be used in the rear-facing position for babies up to 35 pounds). Infant seats hold a baby in a semireclining position and have fold-down handles so that the seat can also be used as a carrier. They can have either three-point (shoulders and crotch) or five-point (shoulders, hips, and crotch) restraints. Three-point restraints require one fewer step to fasten but are not quite as safe as five-point restraints. Some infant car seats buckle directly onto the seat, while others come with a base that buckles in and holds the car seat. A model with a base is very convenient because the seat snaps in and out quickly (while the base remains buckled in), but research indicates that unless the base fits tightly into your car, your child may be safer if you use the seat without the base.

Some parents choose not to invest in an infant car seat and instead opt for a convertible car seat that can be used from birth to 40 pounds. If possible, consider buying an infant car seat—not only because its size is perfectly suited for a small baby, but because it can also be used as a carrier. Young babies sleep a lot, and it's very convenient to be able to take the baby out of the car without having to take him out of the car seat, which is likely to wake him up.

Convertible Car Seats
Age: Birth–4 years

Convertible car seats are for children from birth to 40 pounds. They are used in a semireclining, rear-facing position for babies until they have reached at least one year of age and weigh at least 20 pounds, and in an upright, forward-facing position for toddlers and preschoolers. This type of car seat is secured to the seat of the vehicle by threading a seat belt through its base. The safest front-facing models also have a tether at the top of the seat that secures it to the car. All new car seats are required to come equipped with top tether straps.

There are two types of harnesses available on convertible seats, five-point and three-point.

Five-point harness

This secures the baby at the shoulders, the hips, and the crotch. This system is considered the safest because it can be adjusted closest to the child's body. All higher-end car seats and some lower-priced models have five-point restraints.

Three-point harness

This secures the baby at the shoulders and the crotch. There are two styles of three-point harnesses. On the T-shield model, the shoulder straps meet at a soft plastic T-shaped shield that buckles into the seat base at the child's crotch. The T-shield should be no higher than chest level. The overhead, or bar, shield restraint system has a padded shield that swings over the child's head, drawing the straps over his shoulders. A third strap attached to the shield buckles into the car seat at the crotch. The overhead shield should hit the baby at chest level. Many parents choose three-point systems because they are quick and easy to fasten and unfasten. When used correctly, they provide adequate safety and meet Federal Motor Vehicle Safety Standards (FMVSS).

Whichever type of harness you choose, make sure the shoulder straps are easily adjustable. Not only will you have to regularly adjust the straps as your child grows, but you may have to adjust them depending upon the bulkiness of the clothing he's wearing. Look for straps that adjust by pulling a strap at the crotch rather than a buckle on the back of the seat.

Booster Seats
Age: 4 years and up

When your child reaches 40 pounds, he has outgrown his convertible car seat and is ready to move on to a booster. Although only 22 states and the District of Columbia have laws requiring booster seats for children who have reached the limits of their car seats (usually 4 years or 40 pounds), many recent studies have shown the value of using a booster seat

CAR SEAT INSTALLATION AND SAFETY CHECKLIST

Even though incorrect car seat installation leads to many injuries and deaths every year, studies have shown that fewer than 50 percent of car seats are installed properly. Take the time to read the instruction booklet that comes with your car seat thoroughly to make sure that you are installing and using your seat correctly.

The following checklist highlights the most common car seat safety issues. However, it is not a substitute for reading the manual, because every seat has slightly different features.

- Fill out and mail in your registration card to insure that you will be notified should your car seat be recalled.
- Make sure that the car seat you are using is appropriate for your child's age, height, and weight.
- Babies under one year old must ride facing backward, no matter what they weigh. This is because their neck muscles are not sufficiently developed to hold their heads steady during an impact. Children over one year old who weigh less than 20 pounds should also ride facing backward.
- The safest place for a car seat is in the middle of the back seat, but this is not always possible with the new LATCH system. Properly installed car seats can also be safely positioned on the sides of the second seat or on the third seat of a van (but not on a sideways or backward-facing station wagon jump seat).
- Never place a car seat—or any child age 12 or under—in the front seat of a car with a passenger-side air bag.
- If the seat belt you use to secure your car seat has a free-sliding latch, you must use a locking clip to secure the belt. This is a small metal device that is included with most car seats (look for it taped to the underside or the

---

CAR SEAT INSTALLATION AND SAFETY CHECKLIST
(continued)

---

back of the seat) and can also be purchased separately. A free-sliding latch is one that the seat belt moves through freely, as opposed to one that locks into place when it is adjusted for size. If you can see the seat belt threading through the latch, it is free-sliding; if the mechanism is more like a closed box; it's probably not. If you have any doubt about whether you need to use the clip or questions about installing it, call the manufacturer's help line or your local police or fire department and ask for assistance.

- The base of the car seat should rest firmly on the vehicle's seat and be tightly secured by the seat belt. If the car seat can move more than an inch in any direction, it's too loose.
- It's a good idea to have your installation job checked out by a pro. Call your local police department, fire department, or hospital to see if they hold regular car seat safety check sessions, or visit the NHTSA Web site at www.nhtsa.gov and check out their car seat inspection station locator.

---

until a child is big enough to use the regular lap/shoulder belt correctly. The laws are changing, and using a belt-positioning booster seat is highly recommended until a child is 60 to 80 pounds (depending on his height).

A belt-positioning booster seat has a high, straight back. It has guides on the sides to thread the car's seat belt through, which hold it at a proper position across the child's chest and hips. Some boosters also have a removable five-point harness system to use for a child over four who is between 30 and 40 pounds. Still others have a five-point harness and are marketed as convertible car/booster seats for children 22 pounds and over. Most experts, however, recommend using a regular car seat until a child is at least three years old.

Some companies still offer lap belt-positioning (shield) booster seats that have no back and simply reposition the lap belt across the child's hips. These seats are of questionable value and should not be used in place of a shoulder belt-positioning booster.

Travel Vests

This five-point restraint harness has a padded back and seat and straps into the car using a lap or lap/shoulder belt. Although it is federally approved for use by children from 25 to 40 pounds, it does not protect as well as a car seat or booster seat. Light and packable, travel vests are convenient for taxi rides, rental cars, or car pools but should not be used as a permanent substitute for a car seat or booster.

Car Seat Accessories

Infant head rest

This horseshoe-shaped bolster is attached to a thin fabric pad that is shaped to fit in the car seat. The bolster circles a

---

 PARENTS ALERT

Seat belt positioners: These sleeve-type seat belt positioners, which are supposed to adjust a standard seat belt to fit properly across a child's chest and hips, have been found to be dangerous. The seat belt is threaded through the positioner, which makes the shoulder belt fit across the child's chest rather than his face, but while the positioner lowers the shoulder belt, it also raises the lap belt across the child's abdomen to a position that could lead to internal injuries in a crash. Use a belt-positioning booster seat until your child is big enough for a regular seat belt.

newborn baby's head and keeps it from flopping to the side. This is a must-have item for newborns, and it can also be used in an infant carrier or baby swing.

Neck support
This small pillow has straps that wrap around the car seat straps and attach to them with Velcro to hold a baby or toddler's head upright while he naps. They are not usually necessary once your baby has gained full head and neck control (at about 4 months) and are not as effective as an infant head rest for a newborn.

Back-seat mirror
This mirror attaches to the car's visor or windshield to give you a full view of the back seat. For rear-facing car seats, a mirror that attaches to the back seat allows you to watch your baby in the rear-view mirror.

Seat protector
This rubber, vinyl, or nylon mat is placed on the seat of the car before the car seat is installed. Some protectors have pockets to store gear.

Back-seat organizer
A series of nylon and mesh pockets, the organizer straps onto the back of the front seat and holds bottles, snacks, toys, diapers, books, and other essentials. A cheaper, slightly messier alternative is to keep a big box of toys and books on the seat next to the car seat so your child can simply reach in and choose his own entertainment.

Car seat tote
This carrying case zips around the car seat for protection and ease of handling during travel.

Sunshade
Designed to protect your baby from UV rays, sunshades attach with suction cups onto the inside of your car's back-seat

windows or the back windshield. Some models roll up and down, while others are made of adhesive plastic that sticks to the windows. You'll probably find you need one or two of these if your car doesn't have tinted glass.

Car seat sunshade

This reflective cover is placed over the unoccupied car seat to keep it from heating up when your car does. Draping a blanket or towel over the seat often works just as well, but the sunshade may be better if you live in an extremely hot climate.

Out and About

Eating on the Road

You may need the following paraphernalia to keep your baby well fed while traveling.

Portable feeding seat

Both types—clip-on seats and booster seats with tray—are discussed earlier *(see pages 73–75)*. Clip-on seats are easy to travel with but cannot be used with all tables. Booster seats can be placed on almost any chair, but many of them are bulky. The best alternative for a family that travels a lot may be a folding booster seat with a tray.

Insulated tote bag

Insulated bags keep food and drinks cold for several hours. These bags come in all sizes, from a single-bottle model to a six-bottle cooler with a separate pocket for baby food and utensils. You may want a small one for quick trips and a larger one for more extended travel.

Portable bottle warmer

This clever little device wraps around a bottle or baby food jar and plugs into your car lighter to safely warm it up.

Car seat snack tray

This plastic tray snaps across a forward-facing car seat and allows your child to snack or play in the car.

Food containers

Use small plastic cups or bowls with tight-sealing lids in many sizes instead of plastic bags to transport food if you want it to get where you're going in one piece.

Travel cups

Spill-proof Sippy cups travel well, but even these should be placed in a sealed plastic bag if you're not positive they will stay upright. Cups or canteens with lids or fold-down straws stay the driest of all.

Shopping Cart Restraints
Age: 6 months–3 years

The best advice is don't do it. Thousands of children are injured every year when they fall from a shopping cart, or the cart tips over. Most shopping carts have seat belts, but the thin straps may be too narrow to support an infant, or too flimsy to restrain a toddler. A shopping cart restraint—a nylon pad that covers the cart's seat, with a wide belt that wraps around the child and attaches to the seat behind him—may work better to keep a child from climbing out, but the cart is still at risk of tipping over. If you absolutely can't use a stoller or backpack (or front pack), keep both hands—and your eyes—on the cart at all times.

Safety Tethers
Age: 1 year and up

We all say we'll never do it, but when it comes down either to losing your child in a crowded mall or putting him on a leash, the choice is clear. Some children, once they start walking, are simply not content to stay in a stroller or child carrier for any length of time. In this case, finding a way to keep him close to you in public spaces is necessary. Safety

⚠️ **PARENTS ALERT** ⚠️

Electronic tether: This serves a similar purpose to a tether but is actually an electronic system that sounds an alarm if your child ventures too far away from you. The child wears a small electronic alarm that sounds when he goes out of the range of the monitor the parent carries. Although this system may seem more appealing than a physical tether, it has several flaws. The first is that it may not operate correctly. Another is that the child may remove the sensor without your knowing. Finally, even when the alarm sounds, alerting you that your child is out of range, it doesn't tell you where he is—vital information in a crowded fairground or expansive park. Your best bet is to keep your child physically attached to you.

tethers come in two basic types—wrist band and harness. The harness model is preferable because it can't slip off and can also be used in a stroller, high chair, or shopping cart.

Portable Cribs/Play Yards
Age: Birth–3 years

The portable crib, which doubles as a play yard, is one of the most convenient and versatile baby products around. These enclosures are made of nylon or cotton and mesh over a metal frame that folds down to fit into a carrying case that's about 3 feet long and 10 inches high and deep. Although old-fashioned wooden portable cribs, which fold flat, are still available, they are impractical for traveling and may be rickety and unsafe.

Available in several sizes and shapes, portable cribs offer many different combinations of features. No matter which model you choose, make sure that it assembles and folds down easily (try before you buy—some are much easier to operate than others) and that it has a mechanism to ensure that it cannot compress when the baby is inside. The crib should have no exposed metal parts or sharp edges, and nothing that a baby's fingers or clothes could get caught in. The mesh holes should be one-quarter inch or smaller, and the sides should be high enough to accommodate a child up to 34 inches tall. The mattress (which is included) should attach to the bottom of the crib with Velcro to ensure that the baby cannot become trapped between the mattress and the crib.

A basic portable crib/play yard is rectangular and measures about 2 feet by 4 feet. Larger and smaller versions are available, as are square models and triangular ones that are made to fit into a corner (less room for baby but maximizes your space).

Other options include the following:

- *Wheels.* A handy feature if you plan to move the crib around while it's set up. Make sure the casters lock and the crib is stable.
- *Toy pocket.* A large fabric pocket that attaches to an outside end of the crib with Velcro.
- *Bassinet insert.* A fabric insert that hangs over the top of the crib to create a 6-inch-deep "bassinet" for a newborn baby, which can also be used as a changing surface. The bassinet insert may be included or bought separately.
- *Rocking mechanism.* When engaged, it lets the crib rock from side to side like a cradle. Make sure the rocking bar locks tightly into place.
- *Vibrating mechanism.* Vibrates the crib to soothe newborns.
- *Sunshade.* An arched fabric canopy that fits over the top of the crib for outdoor use.
- *Mosquito netting.* Mesh that fits over the top of the crib to keep insects off the baby.

Travel Beds
Age: 2 years and up

These are for kids who have outgrown the portable crib. One type is a 4-foot-long mat with 4-inch sides that breaks down into a carrying case. The sides are often comforting for children who still like to feel contained in their beds. Other models are simply foam pads that roll up like a sleeping bag.

Sleeping bags

There are many child-sized sleeping bags made for indoor use. Look for one made of soft cotton quilting, cotton jersey, or fleece. The zipper should be plastic, not metal, and sewn in well so it won't snag pajamas or skin.

Travel Toys
Age: Birth and up

Almost any small toy can be pressed into use when necessary, but there are some wonderful playthings that are made specifically for use on the road.

Activity play quilt (Birth–9 months)

For an infant who is not yet mobile, an activity quilt serves two purposes—as a toy to look at and play with, and as a safe, clean surface to lie on wherever you go. Look for one with lots of bright colors and interesting things to touch and observe, and listen to (teether, mirror, rattle, stuffed toy, etc.).

Activity center (2–7 months)

This is an activity quilt with one or two pop-up fabric arches that dangle toys overhead for your baby to bat or grasp. Almost any rattle or small toy can be hung from the arches—change them often to keep your baby interested. When you're ready to move on, the quilt folds flat and the arches serve as handles. There is even an inflatable version. This is an indispensable item for infants on the go.

AIR TRAVEL WITH BABIES

Children under the age of two may fly free on most airlines if you hold your child in your lap. It is safer to buy a seat for each child, and to bring air travel–approved car seats to use on the plane (check the label to make sure). Most airlines offer discounts for under-twos.

If you have more than one child under age two traveling with you, be aware that some airlines require you to have one adult per child in order for the children to fly free. You must buy a seat for each extra child.

Car seat gallery (Birth–6 months)

This is a square of fabric with high contrast graphics that you hang on your car's back seat for your baby to look at. Some models fold into a wedge for floor play. Others have clear pockets that allow you to change the patterns. Many young babies are calmed by looking at these patterns.

Car seat activity toys (3 months–3 years)

These come in several different versions for both infant and toddler car seats. For infants, the toys are hung overhead from a bar or strap attached to the car seat's carrying handle or a foam arch that attaches to the sides of the seat.

For toddlers, there are toy bars that clip to the sides of the seat and fabric arches that are anchored under the car seat. Make sure that any toy you choose moves out of the way easily when you want to remove your child from the seat. Many toddler car bars include a steering wheel and keys as well as squeakers, rattles, and things to twist and turn. Some also have music. Look for a style that allows you to clip on your own toys for variety.

Stroller toy bar (6 months–3 years)
Similar to car seat toy bars, these fit across the front of a stroller and offer a variety of activities. Ones that can be re-configured will hold your child's interest longer than one that is always the same.

Toy links (4 months–2 years)
Plastic links that can be hooked together to form a chain are wonderful for outings. Infants can use the easy-to-grasp links as teethers, while toddlers can practice joining and taking them apart. The links can also be used as a safe tether to attach a toy to a stroller, high chair, or car seat. Look for sturdy links that will not come apart too easily.

Attachable activity toys (6 months–2 years)
These toys are like mini activity boxes, with spinning wheels, clacking noises, and other manipulatives all attached to one hand-held toy. Some also play music. These usually come with a link to attach to a stroller or car seat.

Inflatable beach ball (9 months–3 years)
This is a wonderful toy to take on a trip because it can be packed flat and then blown up once you reach your destination.

Washable crayons and paper (2–3 years)
Little artists will love to create in the car (on a car seat snack tray) or in a high chair in a restaurant. Washable crayons are key at this age.

Board books (9 months–3 years)
Small board books are perfect for toting around in the diaper bag, and they keep toddlers entertained just about anywhere. Bring along a mix of old favorites (children love familiarity and repetition) and new titles (to keep them from getting bored).

Books on tape (18 months–3 years)

Many children's books are now available on tape, and those aimed at the very young often come with a book so they can follow along. *The Cat in the Hat, 101 Dalmatians, Winnie-the-Pooh*, and *The Wind in the Willows* are perennial favorites, as are collections of nursery rhymes and fairy tales.

Chapter 5

Safe and Sound

Our most basic responsibility as parents is to keep our children healthy and safe from harm. It's amazing how difficult this can seem when you're trying to get medicine down the throat of a wailing infant, bathe a squirming newborn, or keep a wily toddler out of the fireplace. The products in this chapter were designed to make keeping your baby safe and sound a bit easier, whether they're used for health, hygiene, childproofing, or safe seating. Accidents can happen, of course, even with the best safety equipment in place. Your best defense—and most important safety measure—is, without doubt, vigilant supervision.

Health

Thermometers
Age: Birth and up

Body temperature can be measured through the mouth, the rectum, the armpit, and the ear. Since it is dangerous to take a temperature orally before a child is five years old, you'll need an accurate thermometer for one (or more) of the other areas. These are your choices.

Standard thermometer

For most of today's parents, a mercury thermometer was a basic item in any medicine cabinet, but they are now discouraged because of concern over mercury as an environmental toxin. While the amount of mercury in an individual thermometer is very small, the amount contained in the fever thermometers sold every year adds up to an estimated 4.3 tons. That's still only a small portion of the mercury in the environment, but phasing out these thermometers is one step toward reducing children's exposure to this hazard.

Digital thermometer

Digital thermometers marketed for babies and children can usually be used orally, rectally, or under the arm. These battery-operated thermometers are unbreakable and register temperature within 30 seconds to 2 minutes (they beep when they're done).

Ear (tympanic) thermometer

This battery-operated thermometer determines body temperature by measuring the infrared heat generated by the ear drum and surrounding tissue, converting it to an oral or rectal equivalent, and displaying it on a screen. The tip of the thermometer has a tiny lens that fits into the opening of the ear canal (it must be held at just the right angle for an accurate reading; this takes a bit of practice). The lens is covered by a plastic filter that is changed each time a new tempera-

ture is taken. Most models have an automatic shutoff feature
to preserve the battery. Some models display temperature
readings in both Fahrenheit and Celsius; some have lighted
displays for nighttime readings; and some have a memory
that records the last eight temperatures taken. Consider the
features that are important to you, and don't pay for any you
won't use. Though pricey, an ear thermometer is a painless
and fairly accurate way to take a baby's or child's temperature that many parents find well worth the investment. Read
the operating directions carefully, and ask your pediatrician
to show you how to use it if you have any questions.

Underarm thermometer

This battery-operated thermometer works much like the ear
thermometer, using infrared sensors to instantly register an
underarm (axillary) temperature. Features (like automatic
shutoff) and price are similar to the ear thermometer, too.
Some parents prefer to take an axillary temperature because
it can be done while the baby is sleeping and can be more
comfortable than an ear thermometer. The readings, however, are not as accurate—they can be up to two degrees low.
You can also use an oral or rectal mercury thermometer to
take an underarm temperature.

Pacifier thermometer

This is just what it sounds like—a digital thermometer built
into a pacifier that measures body temperature orally. Not
the most accurate of thermometers, this works well only if
the baby keeps up a steady sucking motion for at least one
minute (or until the thermometer beeps to let you know it is
finished reading the temperature). Consider a pacifier thermometer a fever screening device rather than an accurate
way to measure body temperature.

Forehead strip thermometer

This small plastic strip is placed on the forehead and held
there for a minute or two as it registers body temperature.
This is not an accurate way to measure a child's temperature

HOW TO TAKE YOUR BABY'S TEMPERATURE WITH A STANDARD THERMOMETER

While the mercury thermometer is being eliminated, it is still the most prevalent—and most accurate—tool for assessing fever, and every parent should know how to use it properly. Whether you're traveling, your battery is dead at three a.m., or your doctor recommends taking a rectal temperature for accuracy, it's good to be armed with the knowledge in advance. And while taking your infant's rectal temperature may seem like cruel and unusual punishment, if it is done correctly, it will hurt you more than it will hurt her.

Before using a standard thermometer, wash it thoroughly with soap and cold water, rinse, then swab it with rubbing alcohol. Next, holding the non-bulb end of the thermometer, shake the mercury below 96 degrees by gently flicking your wrist. It's best to do this over a soft surface like a carpet or bed, in case you accidentally drop the thermometer. Before taking a rectal temperature, lubricate the tip of the thermometer with a little bit of petroleum jelly.

Try to take your baby's temperature when she has been calm for at least half an hour, as crying can raise body temperature (this, of course, may be impossible when a baby is sick and cranky). Lay her over your lap on her belly so that her legs fall at a 90-degree angle and try to distract her by talking or singing in a soothing voice. Use one hand to spread the buttocks, and with the other slip the thermometer gently about one inch into the rectum (never force the thermometer in). Hold the thermometer in place between your index and middle fingers for two to three minutes. Gently remove, wipe the end with a tissue, and read the temperature. Wash the thermometer thoroughly after use.

and should be used only as a screening device—or better yet, not at all. Your hand or lips on your child's forehead will probably give you just as much information.

Humidifiers and Vaporizers
Age: Birth–3 years

Humidifiers and vaporizers are used to add moisture to the air when your baby has a cold, a cough, a sore throat, or the flu. Moist air soothes the mucous membranes throughout the respiratory system, quieting coughs and making breathing more comfortable. Humidified air is also good for moistening skin. Be sure to read the instructions that come with your humidifier or vaporizer carefully and to clean your unit often (daily is best). Do not use these units for extended periods of time, because the moist air may encourage mold growth on your plants, furniture, and other surfaces in your home. Keep the temperature in your home under 68 degrees Fahrenheit during cool months to prevent excessively dry air, and make sure your house is not completely airtight—there should be some way for fresh air to enter and circulate.

There are four types of humidifying devices to choose from, each with its own set of pros and cons.

Cool-mist humidifiers

These can be used year round to maintain a comfortable level of humidity in the air. Water is drawn from a reservoir in the humidifier up through a tube by a spinning propeller. The water is then discharged into the air as a fine mist of droplets. Some parents prefer to use a cool-mist humidifier in their baby's room because there is no risk of scalding if the water spills. Cool water, however, is a breeding ground for germs and molds. A cool-mist humidifier should be cleaned every third day according to the manufacturer's directions and wiped dry. Be sure to rinse the unit several times to make sure there is no leftover cleaning agent that could be dispersed into the air. These humidifiers may also disperse minerals from tap water into the air, which can be dangerous to breathe, so you need to use distilled water with them. Bare-bones humidifiers are fine for occasional use. Available features include a child-resistant switch, a top safety lock, auto stop, and a filter system to extract pollen and dust from the air.

Ultrasonic humidifiers

These humidifiers create a cool mist with ultrasonic sound vibrations. They operate more quietly than cool-mist models and produce much finer droplets of water, so the moisture is distributed more evenly. Like cool-mist humidifiers, however, they are prone to dispersing pollutants and minerals into the air, so they require careful cleaning and use of distilled water.

Steam vaporizers

Vaporizers are best for occasional, short-term use during coughs, colds, sore throats, and the flu. A heating element inside the vaporizer boils the water, which turns into steam that is released into the air. The steam enters the air at a temperature of 170 degrees Fahrenheit, so it is essential to keep the unit out of reach and pointing away from the baby to prevent burns. A vaporizer has the advantage of being less likely to send germs and molds into the air, because most of them are killed when the water is boiled, and you don't have to worry about minerals, either. The unit should be cleaned weekly. Extra features include automatic water cooling, a weighted bottom to discourage tipping, auto stop, and timers.

Evaporative humidifiers

Evaporative units may be the best choice for humidifying, though they do carry a higher price tag. Evaporative humidifiers draw air into a base that has been moistened with water and emit the moistened air in the form of an invisible vapor. Evaporatives disperse less bacteria and molds into the air than cool-mist and ultrasonic humidifiers, but you do need to use distilled water. Features include wicking filters to remove pollutants and bacteria from the air, devices to maintain consistent moisture levels in the room, and ultra-quiet operation.

First Aid
Age: Birth and up

It's best to have first-aid supplies on hand before you need them. Naturally, keep them all out of reach of children. You might want to get a small locked cabinet made for this purpose. Consult your baby's doctor for specific product recommendations and their dosages.

This list of common first-aid supplies will help you get started stocking your medicine cabinet:

- *Liquid aspirin substitute.* Infant acetaminophen (Tylenol, Panadol) or ibuprofen (Advil, Motrin) drops for pain relief and fever reduction. Always use the dropper that comes with the bottle for dosing, and consult your doctor about the correct dosage for your baby—acetaminophen overdosing can cause liver damage. Acetaminophen also comes in rectal suppositories for infants who can't keep a liquid down and toddlers who resist medication.
- *Saline nose drops.* Used to soften secretions in a baby's nose so they can be more easily removed.
- *Antibiotic cream or ointment.* Bacitracin or neomycin. Use on healing circumcision wounds and other cuts and scrapes.
- *Hydrogen peroxide.* For cleaning cuts—less painful than alcohol.
- *Calamine lotion or hydrocortisone cream (½%).* For eczema, rashes, and insect bites.
- *Medicine doser.* Get a dropper or syringe type for infants.
- *Rehydration fluid.* To treat diarrhea. Use only under a doctor's supervision.
- *Rubbing alcohol.* To clean umbilical cord stump and thermometers.

⚠️ **PARENTS ALERT** ⚠️

Baby aspirin: Never give a child aspirin. The use of aspirin with certain viral diseases such as chicken pox and the flu has been linked to the development of Reye's syndrome, a potentially fatal disease. Instead, give your child aspirin substitutes like acetaminophen or ibuprofen to relieve pain and reduce fever. Remember to dose correctly according to your child's weight, not age.

- *Bandages and gauze pads.* Make sure you have some tiny gauze pads as well as larger bandages.
- *Adhesive tape.* For use with gauze pads.
- *Nasal aspirator.* Small bulb syringe used to suction mucous out of the the baby's nose.
- *Ear syringe.* Larger bulb syringe used to remove ear wax. Use only if the doctor recommends it.

As your child grows, be sure to check and restock your first-aid supplies. Throw away medicines that are out of date and add items that are appropriate for each new age and stage. Here are some examples:

- *Sunscreen.* Use a PABA-free one with an SPF of 15 or higher that is especially formulated for babies.
- *Insect repellent.* Check with your baby's doctor about the age to start using this.
- *Medicine doser.* Use a calibrated cup or spoon for toddlers.
- *Decongestant.* Liquid infant formula. Not usually recommended for very young infants. Do not give a decongestant to a child without first consulting your pediatrician.
- *Liquid aspirin substitute.* Switch from infant's to children's formula around age two (upon your doctor's recommendation). Doses are calibrated differently

POISON TREATMENT

Almost everybody has a bottle of syrup of ipecac some-where in the medicine chest to induce vomiting in case of poisoning. But a number of studies have shown that ipecac neither reduces the need for emergency-room treat-ment nor improves the outcome. So toss the ipecac, and keep the nationwide Poison Control Center number handy: 800-222-1222.

(children's formula is less concentrated), so be sure to read the label carefully.

- *Laxatives.* Rarely necessary for breast-fed infants. Older babies and toddlers may sometimes need a gentle laxative. Always consult your baby's doctor be-fore giving laxatives.
- *Tweezers.* For removing splinters and other foreign objects.

Hygiene

Baby Bathtubs
Age: Birth–2 years

There are many different styles of baby tubs on the market, most of which are made to sit on a counter or inside a regu-lar bathtub. Some are contoured to fit into a sink (although none will fit every sink), others convert from infant to tod-dler tubs, and a few even morph into toddler bath seats that suction to the floor of a big tub. When choosing a tub for your newborn, look for a tub that is shaped or padded to hold an infant in a semireclining position. There should be extra support for the head and shoulders. Make sure it has a nonskid bottom and an easily accessible drain. Some tubs fold up, which is great for storage; others have suction cups

Inflatable Tub

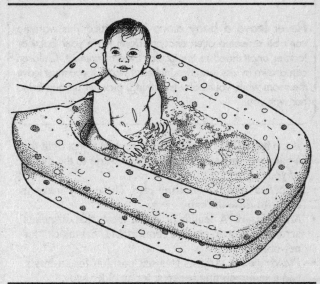

to secure them to a tile or fiberglass wall for easy drying and storing.

One feature to avoid when buying a bath is nonremovable sponge padding. These tend to stay damp and are a breeding ground for mold and mildew. Instead, look for a tub with removable, easily washable padding or a plain plastic model to which you can add a folded towel or large sponge to support your baby. Finally, make sure the tub you choose is large enough for your baby to use until he is about six months old, when he will be able to sit independently and graduate into a bath seat in the big tub.

Here are some other features to consider:

- **Temperature gauge.** Some tubs come with strips or drain plugs that turn a different color when the water

⚠️   **PARENTS ALERT**   ⚠️

Never leave a baby alone in the tub: This warning can't be repeated often enough. Don't leave your baby or toddler unattended in the tub for even a moment. Children can drown in less than two inches of water. If you must leave the room while your baby is bathing, pick her up and bring her with you.

is too hot (90 to 100 degrees Fahrenheit is just right for a baby's bath water—it should feel warm to the inside of your wrist).

- *Attached spray or pouring cup.* These may make it easier to rinse the baby.
- *Mesh insert.* A length of nylon mesh that suspends across the bath to create a comfortable "hammock" for newborns.
- *Plastic insert.* Adjusts to a flat position for an infant and a semireclining backrest for an older baby.
- *Molded convertible tub.* This type of tub is molded to support a reclining infant. Flip it over and it becomes a tub for a seated older baby.
- *Inflatable tub.* This tub sits inside a standard tub and provides a soft, contained bathing space for babies from the time they can sit up on their own. It's also great for travel.

Bath Seats
Age: 6–18 months
Plastic bath seats are for babies who are old enough to sit independently on dry land, but need a bit more support in the water. A baby should not be placed in a bath seat until she has complete head and neck control and can sit unassisted. The seat consists of a plastic bottom that supports a ring inside which the baby sits. The seat secures with suction cups onto the floor of the regular tub (never place a bath seat on a

rubber tub mat or other nonskid surface). Look for a bath seat with a fold-down front that allows for easy entrances and exits. The seat should have enough support to allow the baby to sit without slumping and should hold her in securely enough so that she can't stand up. When inserting the bath seat into the tub, place it out of reach of the faucet.

Bath Accessories and Toys

There are many items available to help you bathe your baby safely and comfortably, and to entertain her during the process. Here are some of the most useful and popular.

Foam insert (Birth to 6 months)

A large, thick sponge with an indentation for the baby to lie on. Good for tubs that don't come with removable padding. Be sure to let the foam dry out between uses to avoid mildew problems.

Bath thermometer (Birth and up)

Lets you know when the water is the right temperature.

Spray hose (6 months and up)

Attaches to your faucet to create a gentle spray that can be directed away from the baby's eyes.

Anti-slip mat (6 months and up)

A must for children once they're out of the baby tub and bath seat. Look for one that is mildew-resistant. Some also have temperature sensors.

Faucet cover (6 months and up)

This plastic or inflatable cover fits over the faucet to protect children from bumps and burns.

Shampoo visor (6 months and up)

Shields the baby's eyes from shampoo when her hair is being rinsed. Can be foam or inflatable.

Toy holder (6 months and up)

Usually attaches to the wall with suction cups. Coated wire is sturdier, but mesh bags tend to stay up better.

Tub mirror (9 months and up)

An unbreakable plastic mirror that attaches to the wall with suction cups and entertains babies. Some have shelves underneath for small toys or toiletries.

Knee and elbow pads (6 months and up)

These ease parents' backs and knees during bath time. One type consists of two cushions (for knees and elbows) connected by a vinyl strip with pouches for storage. The deluxe version is an actual seat with built-in knee and elbow pads. These are for use with standard bath tubs only. The elbow pads are especially useful if your tub has sliding door tracks.

Floating toys (6 months and up)

These can be anything from boats to ducks to little people in life preservers. Babies love to watch them dip and bob. Toddlers use them for pretend play.

Pouring toys (9 months and up)

Any plastic cup or small bucket will do. Cups with holes in the bottom always delight babies.

⚠   **PARENTS ALERT**   ⚠

Sponges and foam toys: Do not give these to an infant or baby, because she may bite off pieces and choke on them. Save sponges and foam toys for children over the age of two.

⚠️ **PARENTS ALERT** ⚠️

Phthalates: Choose hard plastic bath toys rather than soft ones. Some soft plastics contain chemicals called phthalates that some researchers have suggested may be carcinogenic and that may be ingested if a child puts such a toy in her mouth.

Water activity toys (9 months and up)
These toys attach with suction cups to the side of the tub. They include water-activated spinners, squeakers, and detachable pouring toys.

Stick-on letters and shapes (18 months and up)
These foam or vinyl letters and shapes adhere to the sides of the tub or the wall when wet. Don't use the foam type for children under two.

Bath books (6 months and up)
Little vinyl books are fun for the tub. Some include a squeaker.

Bath puppets (6 months and up)
Terry-cloth hand puppets double as washcloths. Make sure any eyes or other decorations are strongly secured.

Bath dolls (18 months and up)
Bath dolls are great tub companions. Make sure the doll is meant to be used in the water and that you dry it well after each use.

Squirting toys (2 years and up)
These soft, squishy animals and other toys are squeezable and squirtable. Don't let kids squirt them into their mouths, though, because mildew can grow inside the toy.

Bath art (2 years and up)

There are many crayons, paints, and gels made for use in the bath. Test each one before you use it to make sure it doesn't irritate your child's skin or stain your fixtures.

Hygiene Products
Age: Birth and up

Soap and shampoo

Doctors recommend using only the gentlest soaps and shampoos on babies. Choose products that are fragrance-free and contain as few additives as possible. Moisturizing soaps are good for keeping a baby's skin from drying out. Soaps do not need to be specially formulated for babies, but it is good to use a no-tears baby shampoo. Most convenient are baby wash products that can be used to wash both body and hair. Pump bottles allow one-handed use.

Toothbrush and toothpaste

It's important to start cleaning your baby's teeth as soon as they appear. First teeth can simply be wiped with a moistened gauze pad every day. As your child gets older, use a small, very soft toothbrush on her teeth and gums. Avoid toothpaste until your child is old enough to understand that it shouldn't be swallowed (around age three). Until that time, brushing with just water is fine. If you do want to use toothpaste for a baby or toddler, choose a children's formula that contains little or no fluoride.

Comb and brush

For a newborn, use a very soft baby brush. As your baby's hair gets longer and stragglier, a combination of combing and brushing will probably work best. Look for soft bristles on brushes and blunt tips on combs. A clean soft toothbrush also works well on wispy baby hair.

Nail clippers or scissors

Get the tiny baby-size and use carefully. Try both clippers and scissors to see which works best for you and your baby.

Potties
Age: 21 months and up

Although some children do learn earlier, most aren't ready to toilet train until they have passed their second birthday, and many (especially boys) are not ready until they are three. It is a good idea, however, to introduce your child to the idea of the potty sometime in the second half of her second year. Start with a one-piece or convertible potty that sits on the floor. This way, your child can explore it and sit on it on her own. Children tend to feel most secure when they can sit with their feet firmly planted on the ground. Let her try it with diapers either on or off, whichever she prefers at first. As she gains confidence and the toilet-learning process progresses, you may want to get a toilet ring as a transitional step from potty to toilet. It's also a good idea to keep a small step stool in the bathroom to help kids use both the toilet and the sink independently.

One-piece potty

These simple, compact potties are made of molded plastic. They are low to the ground and easily portable. They usually have a raised shield between the legs to prevent spraying by boys, so the child must straddle rather than back onto them. Because these potties are one-piece, the whole structure must be washed every time it is used. Many parents find this less convenient than a potty with a removable bowl. If you have a daughter, you may prefer a convertible potty with a removable shield.

Convertible potty

Convertible potties are small and close to the ground (though usually a bit bigger than one-piece potties), so they're easy for young children to use independently. Most have a bowl that can be removed and washed separately and a seat that lifts off and can be placed on top of a regular toilet to make it child-friendly. Some convertible potties also turn into step stools when the seat is removed to give the child a boost up to the big toilet.

Toilet ring

This is a child-sized toilet seat that fits on top of a standard toilet and makes the opening smaller. These are useful both at home and for travel. Toilet rings come with many different features, including padded seats, music, adjustable size (to fit both round and oblong toilets), and built-in step stools. One model folds down into a small plastic bag, and can be carried easily in your pocketbook or diaper bag. Another screws onto the hinge of the toilet lid and flips up and down like a regular toilet seat—a great invention for families who share one toilet.

Step stool

Most children will need help getting onto the toilet until they are about three years old. A bathroom step stool with non-skid feet is a good purchase. Plastic step stools are lightweight and easy for kids to move around. Some even have storage space under the step.

Toilet targets

These ingenious little flushable paper targets encourage little boys to "hit the bull's eye." A few Cheerios thrown into the bowl serve the same purpose.

Potty books and videos

Children seem to be endlessly fascinated with watching and hearing about other children using the potty. Some parents find books and videos helpful in encouraging toilet learning; others see them strictly as entertainment.

Here are some of the best of them:
- *Going to the Potty* by Fred Rogers
- *Once upon a Potty: Boy* and *Once Upon a Potty: Girl* by Alona Frankel
- *The Princess and the Potty* by Wendy Cheyette Lewison
- *Your New Potty* by Joanna Cole
- *It's Potty Time* (Learning through Entertainment)

Training Pants
Age: 2 years and up

When you begin toilet teaching in earnest, you may want to consider using cloth training pants rather than disposables. Although the mess and laundry burden will be greater, there's a good chance that using cloth will shorten the training process significantly (if your child is truly ready, of course). This is because disposable training pants feel like diapers (a wad of paper between the legs) and absorb like diapers (so the child feels little wetness against her skin), so they are usually used like diapers. Cloth training pants, on the other hand, become very cold and uncomfortable when wet, which serves as both an incentive to stay dry and a powerful lesson in what it feels like to have to go. Children in disposable training pants may feel so dry that they never even realize when they urinate.

When you buy training pants, look for styles made of absorbent cotton with a padded, reinforced crotch. Make sure they fit well, too. You won't need to leave room to grow, since you'll (hopefully) be using these for a relatively short time. Wash training pants in the hot cycle in the washing machine.

Safety

Babyproofing
Age: 5 months and up

The minute your baby becomes mobile, she becomes a constant hazard to herself and to anything breakable in your home. The time to begin babyproofing your house is before you think you need to. That way, you won't be caught by surprise by, for example, a five-month-old who can suddenly roll across the room and put her finger in an electric outlet or a seven-month-old who drags herself across the kitchen floor and opens a cabinet full of cleaning supplies.

There are certain babyproofing items that no home with a

mobile baby should be without. These include outlet covers, stair gates, and cabinet locks. On the other hand, it doesn't make sense to go out and buy every babyproofing item imaginable before you know what mischief your baby is likely to get into. Some babies touch almost nothing and seem to have a heightened sense of physical danger. Others can dismantle practically anything in the blink of an eye. Still others seem to be drawn to sharp corners. Most fall somewhere in between. Don't pad and gate everything in your house until you know what type of baby you're dealing with. Another point to consider: Having babyproofing supplies in place means nothing if you don't use them properly. Overloading your home with babyproofing items can potentially lead to heightened danger for your baby, because it's likely you won't actually relatch every gate and door, or you'll forget that you've left something undone. Install babyproofing devices as needed; going overboard may actually backfire.

Here is a list of babyproofing products broken down by degree of necessity. And remember, no babyproofing product can replace the best safety tactic of all: ever-attentive supervision.

Must-haves
Gates
Safety gates are invaluable for preventing your baby from entering unsafe areas of the home. Gates are used between rooms and at the top and bottom of staircases. Gates can be made of wood, plastic, coated metal, or mesh, and they should come with a JPMA seal.

There are two basic types of safety gates, pressure-mount and wall-mount. Pressure-mount gates are not attached to the wall but have two locking panels that adjust to the dimensions of the doorway, and a locking mechanism that supplies the force to hold the gate in place. These gates are for use between rooms and at the bottom of stairs. They can be used only between two smooth, even surfaces.

GATE SAFETY

Safety gates are excellent childproofing devices, but it is imperative that they be installed correctly and used properly. Always read the instructions carefully before using a gate, and keep the following safety points in mind:

- Never place a pressure-mount gate at the top of a stairway. Instead, opt for a wall-mount gate, which is sturdier.
- Install gates with the locking mechanism or bar facing away from the baby.
- Be sure wall-mounted gates are well anchored in a wall stud.
- Always close a gate behind you.
- Discontinue use when your child is 36 inches tall or two years old (the age at which most children are capable of climbing over gates). The gate should never be shorter than three-quarters of the child's height.

Wall-mount gates screw into the wall on one side and connect to a screwed-in latch on the other. This is the strongest type of gate and, if installed correctly, can be used at the top of stairs and in front of windows.

Both pressure-mount and wall-mount gates come in many different styles and with features to suit a variety of needs:
- Step-through gates have a door that swings on a hinge in one or both directions, so the gate doesn't need to be removed each time an adult or older child wants to walk through. Many can be operated with one hand. There are even foot-operated gates. Some close automatically. Some also have a safety bracket that prevents the gate from opening over a stairway.
- Some wall-mount gates can be attached to metal railings or other uneven surfaces.

- Extensions allow some gates to be used in areas over 42 inches wide.
- Extra-long gates fit openings up to 13 feet.
- Some gates can be configured to fit irregularly shaped areas.
- All mesh gates roll up for easy portability (although they may not be strong enough for everyday use).

Cabinet and drawer latches

These are designed to prevent cabinets and drawers from being opened by curious toddlers. The most common (and inexpensive) type consists of a plastic hook that is pushed down with a finger to allow adult access. The hook catches on a latch if it is not depressed. Some latches have an extra safety measure that ensures that the drawer or cabinet will not close on the child's fingers.

Another type of safety latch is a lock that is operated with a magnetic key. The lock can also be temporarily disengaged for easy access. This is an ingenious system, but it only works if you keep track of the key (which is another item that must be stored out of reach of the child).

Cabinet slide lock

This sliding lock secures two cabinets whose handles or knobs are side by side. The lock is placed around the knobs or through the handles and is secured with a sliding latch. An adult can slide the latch off by pushing in the two side buttons. This is a must-have for the cabinets under the kitchen sink.

Toilet latch

Keeps toilet lids down. The best kind locks automatically when the lid is lowered but is easily unlocked by an adult.

Outlet covers

These small plastic caps slide into unused electrical outlets and block probing fingers. More convenient—but much more expensive—are sliding outlet covers. These replace regular electrical outlet plates and slide shut when not in use.

Furniture brackets
These brackets attach heavy furniture like bookcases to the wall so they can't tip over if a child climbs on them. Follow the directions carefully when installing.

Items to consider
Window guards
If you live above the first floor and keep your windows open, consider guarding them with a metal gate specifically made for the type of windows you have (double hung, casement, etc.). When installed properly, these inexpensive devices can save lives. Depending on local laws, landlords may be required to provide and install them.

Doorknob covers
These keep toddlers from entering off-limits rooms and from locking themselves in. Adults firmly push in the two buttons on the side while turning the knob.

Appliance latches
These straps attach with heavy-duty adhesive to keep refrigerators, freezers, and microwave oven doors closed. They also work on dishwashers and trash compactors, but these appliances usually have built-in locks.

Stove knob covers
These plastic covers prevent children from touching the stove knobs.

TV guard
This plastic shield slides under the TV and blocks the control panel but still allows the remote to work.

VCR guard
This plastic device fits into the VCR's opening and prevents fingers, food, and toys from entering.

Cord roller
This device rolls a long electrical cord (up to eight feet) into a plastic case to keep it out of the way.

Cord-control kit
This flexible tubing covers multiple electrical cords and conceals them from children. In addition to their safety function, they help provide clutter control.

Power strip cover
This plastic case fits around a surge suppressor so the plugs cannot be removed.

Hearth guard
This dense foam strip attaches to the edge of a stone or brick hearth to cushion sharp surfaces.

Edge guard
Similar to the hearth guard, this foam strip fits around the edge of a coffee table. It's especially useful for glass tables.

Safety straps
These adhesive straps secure electronic devices like computers, stereos, and TVs so they can't be pulled down.

Balcony guard
A sheet of clear plastic that attaches to a railing to block the spindles of indoor balconies, lofts, and landings. Prevents children from throwing objects over the edge, using the spindles as footholds to climb over the railing, or getting their heads caught between the spindles.

Deck guard
Similar to the balcony guard, but for outdoor use, this plastic netting is designed to block unsafe railings.

Driveway gate
This freestanding net spans the width of a driveway, deterring motorists and reminding kids not to go into the street. This does not substitute for adult supervision, as a child could crawl or walk around it.

Warning signs
These freestanding yellow plastic signs alert motorists that there are children playing nearby.

Automatic door closer
This spring-loaded device attaches to the door jamb and automatically closes interior doors. This is particularly useful if you have an older child who forgets to close basement, bathroom, or garage doors behind him.

Bifold door lock
This plastic clip fits over the top of bifold doors to prevent them from opening. It is easy to remove but not handy for doors you use every day.

Sliding door lock
These plastic stoppers adhere to a sliding door and prevent the other door from sliding over it.

Finger guard
This small plastic device fits over the top or side of a door, keeping it from closing completely to protect fingers from getting caught between the door and the frame.

Window blind cord shortener
Window blind cords roll into this device, so they do not dangle within reach of children. The spool inside lets you pull down or retract the cord by pushing a button.

Door positioner
This small, flexible arch fits under the door to keep it from moving. Pushing the door over the stop locks it into place. When you want to move the door, just step on the positioner to release it.

Door lock release
This device replaces the strike plate on a door. The beauty of this particular item is that it allows the door to be locked and unlocked regularly but also allows it to be opened with a forceful push by an adult, so a child cannot be locked inside.

Hinge locks
These metal locks are installed on the hinge side of a door jamb and flip open and closed to lock or unlock a door. These are great for doors with no locks and much less obtrusive than other alternatives, like hook-and-eye latches.

Items you probably won't need
Oven lock
Many ovens, dishwashers, and trash compactors come equipped with their own locks. You might need an extra latch if yours doesn't, or if your child figures out how to open the built-in lock.

Stove guard
This clear plastic shield keeps children from pulling pots off the stove or touching burners. Turning pot handles inward is usually all that's necessary.

Corner guard
These plastic guards can help protect against especially sharp corners. Soft bumper pads offer more cushioning as a nice alternative.

Fire Safety
Age: Birth and up

The best fire safety strategy is, of course, prevention. Keep matches and lighters hidden and out of your child's reach. If you smoke, immediately dispose of all ashes and cigarette butts, and keep matches and cigarettes out of your child's sight and reach. Never smoke in bed or when you're tired (better yet, don't smoke at all). Here's what you need to make your home as fire safe as possible.

Smoke detector

These should be on every level of your home (including the basement) and near every bedroom. Make sure batteries are fresh and functioning (check and replace them every six months—in the spring and fall when you change your clocks to help you remember). Consider an alarm with a lithium battery, which can last up to ten years. The newest solution is to use household electric current to power smoke detectors. However, since a fire may trip your household circuit breakers, it's wise to have battery back-up.

Fire extinguisher

Get fire extinguishers that are rated ABC, which means they work on all types of fires. Keep one in the kitchen, in the basement, in the garage, and near bedrooms. Keep them out of reach of children. Buy a new fire extinguisher after using it, and have the gauges checked twice a year to make sure they are full and the contents are pressurized.

Fire ladder

If your bedrooms are above ground level, store a collapsible fire ladder in each one. Also, devise an emergency fire escape plan and practice it with your children.

Window decal

Often called "tot finders" or "tot spotters," these decals alert emergency workers to the presence of children in a room. Place one on each window of your child's room and one on the bottom of the door. Use your judgment when using these decals, however. Some experts feel that identifying a child's room indicates easy points of entry for prowlers.

Environmental Safety
Age: Birth and up

Environmental hazards can pose serious risks to everyone, but especially babies and young children, because their bodies are growing and developing so rapidly. It's tempting to ignore or deny environmental risks because they are usually invisible. But for your baby's sake, don't bury your head in the sand. Many environmental hazards can be removed or managed once they're identified. Some, like nitrates and bacteria in drinking water, require professional testing. Others you can test or screen for yourself. If any of these screening tests produce positive results, professional diagnosis and abatement are required.

Carbon monoxide

This odorless, colorless, tasteless gas is produced as a by-product of combustion and is extremely poisonous. Improperly vented fuel-fired furnaces, gas dryers, fireplaces, gas stoves, and automobiles can all produce dangerous levels of carbon monoxide. Carbon monoxide is easily identified by carbon monoxide detectors, which plug right into an electrical outlet and sound an alarm if levels of the gas get high. The Consumer Product Safety Commission advises that every home have a detector mounted near the bedrooms and in utility areas. Follow the manufacturer's instructions carefully when installing your detectors. Carbon monoxide detectors are available at hardware, variety, and many juvenile stores.

Radon

Another odorless, colorless, tasteless gas, radon increases the risk of lung cancer in people who have been exposed to elevated levels over long periods of time. Radon is a naturally occurring radioactive gas that is produced in the soil and leaks into homes through cracks in the foundation. Radon problems are most common in the Northeastern part of the United States. The only way to know whether your home has radon is to test it, either professionally or with a home test kit. Home tests are easy to use—you simply expose them to the air in your basement or the lowest level of your home for a few days and then send the test to an EPA-licensed lab for analysis. The EPA recommends that apartment dwellers who live below the third floor should have their apartments tested for radon as well. If you live in an apartment, ask the landlord if the building has been tested. If it has, ask to see the results. If it hasn't, you can ask to have it done, or do it yourself. You can get radon testing kits in hardware stores, through safety catalogues, or from the National Safety Council. Apartment dwellers can refer to the the Environmental Protection Agency's "A Radon Guide for Tenants."

Lead in water

Lead exposure is dangerous to children, resulting in learning disabilities, attention deficits, hyperactivity, and other neurological problems. Lead in drinking water usually comes from old lead plumbing rather than from the water itself. Home test kits allow you to collect several samples of your water and send them to an EPA-certified lab for analysis. If you have any suspicion of lead in your water, don't use it to drink, cook, or make baby formula until it is tested and cleared or treated. Some filters are excellent at removing lead from water, but you must be sure the kind you get doesn't just improve the taste and odor of water, and you must change the filter regularly. Before treating the water, it is a good idea to find out what the lead levels are. For more information, call the EPA's Safe Drinking Water Hotline.

Lead in household objects

Lead is often found in soil and in paint and pottery glazes. Lead may also be found in the dust from natural disintegration of certain imported vinyl mini-blinds made before 1997. Other sources of lead include lead-based paint, which was used in homes and apartments built before 1978, as well as old painted toys and furniture. Home test kits are available to test for lead in soil, toys, paint, dishes, pottery, and blinds. The results are immediate and do not need to be sent to a lab for analysis. If your home test comes out negative and you still suspect that there may be lead, have the object professionally tested. You can find lead testing kits at hardware and housewares stores and through catalogues. For more information, call the National Lead Information Center.

Asbestos

Asbestos, a material resistant to fire and acid, was used in the construction of insulation, heating ducts, and ceiling

---

GUIDE TO ENVIRONMENTAL SAFETY RESOURCES

EPA's Asbestos in Your Home
http://www.epa.gov/asbestos/ashome.html

EPA's A Radon Guide for Tenants
http://www.epa.gov/iaq/radon/pubs/tenants.html

EPA's Safe Water Information
http://www.epa.gov/safewater/lead/lead1.html
800-426-4791

National Lead Information Center
http://www.epa.gov/opptintr/lead/nlic.htm
800-424-LEAD

National Safety Council (radon information)
800-557-2366
http://www.nsc.org/ehc/radon.htm

tiles prior to 1970. Asbestos has been found to cause cancer and other types of lung disease when its dust is inhaled over time. This dust is especially dangerous for children because their bodies do not filter it out well. Asbestos is most harmful if it is disturbed by touching, sweeping, vacuuming, or the like. It is typically found in the basements of older homes, insulating the hot water pipes. It is usually not harmful to adults if it is not disturbed. If, however, your child goes into the basement, or near any other source of asbestos, you should have the area professionally tested, and the asbestos should be removed by an EPA-certified remediator or professionally encapsulated so the particles cannot escape. For more information, see the EPA's Web site "Asbestos in Your Home."

Microwaves

Some older or damaged microwave ovens leak radiation into the air. Older microwaves are more likely to leak because new ones have to pass tests before they are sold. A home test kit consists of a device that, when held in front of the running microwave, signals with a red or green light whether the radiation is at a safe or unsafe level. Microwave testing kits are available in hardware stores and through catalogs. If your microwave leaks, you can either replace it or get a new seal—which may or may not be worth it, depending on the value of the microwave. If you have any doubts about your microwave, do the test—it's easy and cheap.

Seating and Enclosures

At every age and stage, your baby needs safe places to sit and watch the world go by. The products in this section serve two purposes: to contain and to entertain. Use all of them with care and according to the manufacturer's directions. Never leave a baby unsupervised in any of these. And never leave an unhappy baby trapped in a seat she doesn't want to be in (unless it is for her own safety for a very limited period of time).

Infant Seats
Age: Birth to 6 months

Often called bouncers or rocking seats, infant seats are indispensable for the first six months of a baby's life. They
provide a safe, comfortable place for the baby to sit semi-
upright and, in time, to bounce and play with small toys. Infant seats are lightweight, portable, and can be used in any
room or outdoors.

Most bouncers consist of a fabric seat suspended from a
metal or plastic frame. When the baby moves, the seat re-
sponds with a soft bouncing motion that most babies find
very soothing. Look for a bouncer with a wide, stable base
and nonskid bottom. Some have inserts like those for car
seats to keep your baby's head from falling to the side,
though this is not essential. Never leave your baby in the seat
unattended or place it on a raised or slippery surface.

Look for the following features:

- *Vibrator.* Battery-operated vibrating seats are often
  comforting to cranky or colicky babies. Some babies,
  however, find the vibrating motion distressing.
- *Toy bar.* Most seats come with a removable toy bar.
  Babies enjoy looking at the toys even before they're
  able to bat or reach for them.
- *Canopy.* A canopy is nice if you use the seat outdoors.
- *Portability.* The ability to fold up is good if you plan to
  transport the seat often.
- *Convertible rocker.* Some seats convert from rockers
  to stationary bouncers.

Convertible Bassinets/Bouncers
Age: Birth to 6 months

A convertible bassinet/bouncer is a small bassinet that rests
on a metal bouncer frame. This device can be used anywhere
you would use a bouncer, but it is mainly intended for outdoor
use. Unlike a regular bouncer, the bassinet/bouncer has sides.
It also has a large canopy that meets a netting canopy (raised

from the foot of the device) and zips together for complete protection from sun and insects. A vibrating version is also available. This is a must-have for summer newborns who will spend a lot of time sleeping at the beach or pool.

Support Pillows
Age: 5 months and up

A support pillow is shaped like a horseshoe and is densely stuffed to make it very firm. Its purpose is to help support the baby as she learns to sit up—the baby is seated in the middle of the hole with her back and shoulders supported by the pillow. It's also a handy safety device for newly independent sitters to cushion occasional falls. Many mothers use these cushions as nursing pillows for the first few months. They can also be pressed into service as floor cushions for older babies and children.

Baby Swings
Age: 6 weeks–8 months

Baby swings are true saviors for exhausted parents who feel that they will collapse if they have to walk the floor for another minute with a crying baby in their arms. Most babies love the gentle rocking motion of the swing and calm down immediately when placed in it. Baby swings come in two basic types: wind-up and battery operated. Wind-up swings are powered by cranking, which keeps the swing in motion for 10 to 15 minutes, depending on how much you wind it. Battery-operated swings run until they are switched off. Although the battery-operated models cost a bit more, they are well worth the price. Wind-up swings not only stop without warning but also tend to be noisier and move less smoothly.

Although baby swings can be lifesavers, they should be used with certain precautions in mind. Always strap your baby into the swing (even if it has a tray restraint, too), and never leave her swinging unattended. Make sure the swing is stable, and follow the manufacturer's weight and age guidelines. Never hang toys from the swing, because they could get tangled in the mechanism or pose a strangulation risk. Finally, although the temptation may be great, don't overuse the swing. Babies of all ages need a lot of human contact and shouldn't be left swinging—even if they seem content—for hours on end.

When you're shopping for a baby swing, consider these features:

- *Open top.* This feature allows you to easily place the baby in and out of the swing without worrying about hitting her head on an overhead crossbar.
- *Removable seat.* Some swing seats can be removed from the frame and used as portable infant seats.
- *Variable speeds.* Gentle swinging is appropriate for newborns, while some older babies prefer a faster motion.
- *Cradle.* Cradle attachments allow you to swing your baby lying down—making it possible to use the swing from birth.
- *Timer.* Some swings come equipped with a timer that stops the swing gradually after a certain length of time.
- *Removable, washable cover.* A convenient feature of most swings.
- *Music.* Some swings feature built-in music boxes.
- *Toys.* Some swings have small toys attached to the lap tray. Don't buy or use a swing that has dangling toys (some older models do).

Doorway Jumpers
Age: 4–8 months
Jumpers are another device aimed at containing and entertaining pre-locomotive babies. A jumper is a fabric seat suspended from a plastic frame which is in turn suspended from straps and a large spring or bungee cord. The apparatus clamps above the molding at the top of a doorway (you cannot hang a jumper in a doorway without a molding). The

baby hangs in the seat in an upright position with her feet on the floor. The pressure on the soles of the feet encourages the baby to bounce up and down, an activity that many babies love (but some do not). The plastic frame around the seat should have bumpers to soften any bumps against the door frame.

A baby should not be placed in a jumper until she has full head and neck control (usually at four or five months). As with all seating devices, a child should never be left in a jumper unattended. The manufacturer's instructions and weight limits should be followed strictly. Some doctors believe that using a jumper can be harmful to a baby's joints because of the high impact of the bouncing motion. There has not been enough proof, though, to have jumpers removed from the market, so parents should use them at their discretion.

Stationary Entertainers
Age: 4–10 months
Stationary entertainers are the next generation of walkers—basically, walkers that don't move. Instead, the baby is entertained by an array of attached toys and activities and by the rocking or bouncing motion of the base. The entertainer (or exerciser) is a swiveling fabric seat suspended from a plastic frame that rests on a base that may be either flat or bowl shaped. The flat-bottomed version has springs and bounces; the bowl-bottom version rocks.

Most babies enjoy the upright position that the entertainer affords them. They can sit or stand in the seat and play with both manipulative and noise-making toys. Some entertainers have a battery and feature lights and music. Others have unusual things to gaze at, like a rubber duck floating under a plastic dome. Look for an entertainer with a removable, washable seat and legs that can be easily adjusted to accommodate babies of different heights. As with any seating device, do not leave your baby in it unsupervised, and always take her out at the first sign of boredom or displeasure.

Stationary Entertainer

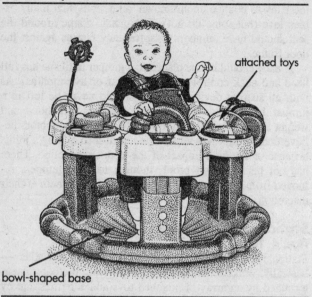

attached toys

bowl-shaped base

Play Yards
Age: 3 months–2 years

A play yard (formerly known as a playpen) can be used indoors or out to safely contain your child. Many babies are quite content to play in a play yard for a limited period of time as long as they have interesting toys to occupy them. Some babies, however—especially older ones—dislike being contained and do not do well in a play yard. To avoid this problem, start familiarizing your baby early, with five- to ten-minute play yard sessions from the age of about three or four months.

Remember that play yards, like all baby equipment, are not supposed to substitute for high-quality adult supervision. So use them judiciously and for limited time periods. While

⚠ **PARENTS ALERT** ⚠

Walkers: Walkers, which consist of a seat within a framework with four wheeled legs, offer babies freedom of movement before they are developmentally ready to handle it. The result is over 24,000 injuries annually that require medical attention. Although walkers are still available, they are fast losing popularity in favor of the newer stationary exercisers. Some parents elect to put their baby in a walker under close supervision, but walkers are best avoided completely.

some parents elect not to use a play yard at all, others find them very helpful for keeping their baby safe while they cook, use the bathroom, garden, or do other household tasks that do not lend themselves to having a baby underfoot. Play yards are also excellent for protecting babies from overzealous older siblings.

Although old-fashioned nonportable mesh playpens are still available in some places, they offer no advantages over portable play yards (which can also be used as portable cribs) and have the disadvantage of being heavy, unwieldy, and hard to store. Most families will find a portable play yard to be an excellent investment that will last through all of their children. *(For a complete description of this type of play yard, see pages 114–115.)*

Activity Yards
Age: 6 months–3 years
An activity yard—sometimes called a kiddie corral—is a super-sized play yard that consists of six steel or plastic panels connected to form a large hexagon. It has no floor and can be used indoors or out. The mesh panels interlock to form a large play area about twice the size of a standard play yard. Additional panels can be added to provide even more play space. This type of play yard is more like a fence that encloses a play area, so children may tolerate it better. It's

also excellent for two or three children together—but be sure they're closely supervised. When the activity yard is not in use, the panels stack and connect for storage.

For the ultimate in play yard entertainment, there are activity yards that have toys such as mirrors, spinners, and squeaky toys built right into the sides. You'll pay more for less space with this type of yard, but many children—and adults—find their toys and bright colors very appealing.

Chapter 6

Play

The greatest thing about being a kid is that it's so much fun. And that's one of the best things about being a parent, too. Almost from birth, a baby engages in play that entertains, stimulates, and helps both his mind and his body grow. Selecting playthings—from toys to books to music to software—can be confusing because there are so many choices available. Some toys and media—like those with dangerous parts, violent or intolerant themes, or gender stereotypes—can be edited out immediately. Classics such as plush animals, lightweight balls, building blocks, and Mother Goose should be a part of every childhood. It's the thousands of toys, books, and CDs in between that present the challenge: choosing quality playthings that will engage your baby beyond the first half hour.

Toys

This chapter aims to help you make selections that will satisfy both you and your baby. It highlights toys that are not only valuable for your baby's physical, intellectual, and social development, but that he will really like, too. Choosing toys, books, and music is, of course, a highly personal process, but the input included here from many experienced parents and professional testers should help point you in the right direction.

Selecting toys for your baby is a lot of fun, and it's easy to get carried away. Here are a few words of advice for parents just starting to build a collection of toys for their baby.

Choose quality over quantity

Although it's good to have a nice selection of toys for your baby to choose from, too many at once will overwhelm him and may actually cause him to lose interest in playing with much of anything. Rotating toys by putting some away to take out at a later date is a tried-and-true strategy for maintaining your baby's interest (and keeping your house from being overrun).

Make sure it's age appropriate

Follow the manufacturer's age guidelines—there's a reason they exist. Never give a child under three years old any toy with small parts that he could choke on. Beyond that, toys meant for much older children are developmentally inappropriate and will frustrate your baby. Even if your child seems advanced, try not to choose toys recommended for kids more than six months beyond his age.

Don't get bogged down by so-called educational toys

With a few obvious exceptions, all toys are educational in some way. Don't feel that every toy in your child's collection specifically has to teach him about colors, shapes, letters, or numbers. Toys teach more subtle things, too, like cause and effect, object permanence, rhythm, societal roles, humor, and emotions. A well-rounded playroom and library is your best goal.

Choose playthings that encourage creativity

While all toys can be used imaginatively by a resourceful child, some are better at fostering creativity than others. Look for toys that encourage open-ended play like balls, blocks, dolls, cars, stuffed animals, pretend food, and water toys. Choose activity toys that offer options rather than just a single way to play, like a shape sorter with dump-and-fill building blocks or an electronic instrument that allows the child to create his own music rather than just listen to prerecorded songs. And remember, the simplest toys are often the most versatile. Don't push your child to use a toy the "right" way; your child will stretch his imagination by investigating all the ways that an object can be used.

Here's a rundown of toys to look for—and a few to avoid—for every stage during the first three years.

Toys for Newborns
Age: Birth–4 months

For your baby's first four months, he will not so much play with toys as gaze, and later bat, at them. Toys for the early months (before a baby learns how to reach and grasp) should stimulate the senses—patterns to look at, soft music to listen to, interesting textures to touch. It's not necessary to have many toys during this period, but there are a few things that stimulate and entertain even the newest baby.

Mobiles

Babies are fascinated by the sights and sounds of a mobile hanging overhead. Newborns will respond first to high-contrast black and white or primary colors. Choose a mobile that is attractive from the baby's perspective—the patterns and faces should be face downward. Remove the mobile from the crib as soon as the baby is able to sit up.

Pattern toys

Newborns love to gaze at high-contrast black-and-white graphic patterns. There are many toys on the market that take advantage of this fact. Some of the best for newborns include cloth or vinyl books that can be set up in the crib or on the floor, a set of patterns that attaches to the back seat of a car so an infant in a rear-facing car seat can gaze at it, and a pattern wedge that sits on the floor.

Musical toys

Soft music soothes babies as well as stimulates their sense of hearing. Some of the best musical toys for this age are "pull-downs"—plush toys that can be hung from the crib rail. When the handle is pulled down, music plays and the toy scrunches up again, accordion-style. This type of toy is also great later on, when the baby can learn to pull it himself.

Plastic music boxes that attach to the crib rail come in many different styles. Some have twinkling lights or even project a light show on the ceiling or wall. Others can be activated by the baby kicking a key pad. The best innovation in music boxes is remote control, which allows you to turn the unit on or off without entering your sleeping baby's room and possibly waking him.

Crib mirrors

Crib mirrors are wonderful for newborns and older babies, too. Look for one that attaches securely to the crib rail and is distortion free. Wedge-shaped mirrors that can be set on the floor in front of the baby are also excellent. Crib mirrors are usually made of metal with a plastic or padded fabric frame.

Floor gyms

Floor gyms are arches with dangling toys. You lie your infant under the arch on his back. At first the baby will just look at the toys, but by about two months he will begin to bat at them. Floor gyms come with an array of features, such as music, lights, and character toys. The best floor gyms are versatile and allow you to hang a variety of toys, which can be rotated. Most convenient are soft fabric floor gyms that come attached to a play mat and fold up for easy transporting.

Activity mats

These are soft quilts for baby's floor time. Either black and white or brightly colored, these mats feature different patterns to look at, textures to explore, and small attached toys, like squeakers and soft animals. The best activity mats are easily machine washable and fold up compactly for travel.

Rattles

Although your baby won't be able to manage a rattle himself until he is about five or six months old, he may enjoy watching and listening to you shake a soft rattle now. Rattles with chiming sounds are especially nice for a tiny baby. Rattles attached to booties or Velcro bracelets may look cute, but they are too heavy for newborns.

Toys for Infants
Age: 5–12 months

As your baby develops from a largely horizontal being to one who can sit upright with his hands free, the play opportunities increase immensely. Around the age of five months, your baby also will learn directed reaching and will be able to grasp objects for extended periods of time. This is the golden age for rattles, huggables, board books, and early manipulatives. Add toys to your baby's collection gradually, noting which types of things hold his interest. As your baby begins to handle his own toys, there are also some things to avoid. These include old toys, which may contain lead paint; foam toys, which can be bitten and choked on; toys with elastic, ribbons, or buttons; and any toys with small parts.

Rattles and teething toys

Your baby will love bright, lightweight rattles with interesting sounds and textures to explore. Look for soft fabric or smooth plastic rattles that have no loose parts and are safe to chew on. Babies this age usually prefer colorful rattles with lots of jiggling beads and gummy textures to plush rattles in muted pastels. Make sure the rattles are small and light enough for young babies to grasp easily. Another variation on the rattle are high chair activity toys that attach to the tray with suction cups and feature spinning, clacking, and rattling parts.

Balls

Babies love to grasp, roll, and chase soft, lightweight balls. Look for balls made of fabric, vinyl, or very lightweight plastic for this age group—never foam. Features such as different textures, chimes or rattles, or twinkling lights add another dimension to this classic toy.

Huggables

Babies love to hug and chew on soft stuffed animals and dolls, but many are inappropriate for this age. Avoid dolls and plush toys with fuzzy fur that could shed or eyes, ribbons, buttons, or small plastic parts that could be pulled off. Infant huggables should be small enough to be handled easily. They should be securely sewn and constructed of washable fabric such as velour or terry cloth. Look for interesting textures, easy-to-grasp shapes, stitched-on features, and sound effects sewn securely inside.

Manipulatives

As your baby develops, his ability to manipulate objects grows by leaps and bounds. Some of the best manipulatives for infants are those that teach cause and effect, including pop-up boxes (when the baby pushes a button or pulls a lever, an animal pops up), electronic toys that make sounds when buttons are pushed (toy phones and radios are must-haves), spinning toys, and simple stacking and nesting toys like cups or boxes. Most babies under a year old do not, however, have the dexterity to stack graduated rings on a post.

Rolling toys and vehicles

Newly crawling babies love to push around rolling toys and easy-to-handle vehicles. Make sure cars and trucks are big and chunky and have no small parts that can be pulled off. This is not the time for diecast metal cars—the wheels detach easily and are the perfect size for choking.

Fill-and-dump toys

Babies love to fill up containers and dump them out—over and over and over again! There are many toys to choose from that encourage this activity, including containers of small plastic blocks, lightweight balls, and textured rings. Babies this age are not yet ready to fit shapes through like-shaped holes (although some can handle slots near the end of the first year). Fill-and-dump toys for babies should feature wide-open containers and easy-to-handle, soft, safe pieces.

Bath toys

As soon as a baby can sit independently in the bathtub, he's ready for the wonderful world of bath toys. Baby tub toys should be big, chunky, and easy to clean. Look for boats with stacking blocks; animals that stack or nest (and, of course, float); cups, sieves, and other pouring toys; and bright vinyl books.

Board books

At this age, books are also toys—great for developing manipulative and fine-motor skills as well as visual discrimination. Provide your baby with plenty of cloth or sturdy cardboard books that he can stack, throw, and "read." You might find him sitting and reading in his own language, in imitation of his reading sessions with you.

HOMEMADE FUN

Did you know that you probably already own some of the best baby toys around? Babies love to play with household objects—sometimes even more so than with expensive toys. Maybe this is the case because they see you using these things and want to imitate you. Here's a list of equipment for safe and fascinating homemade fun for babies six months to three years old:

- Plastic food storage containers and lids
- Plastic measuring cups
- Plastic measuring spoons
- Small saucepans and lids
- Wooden spoons (short-handled)
- Colanders
- Plastic cups and bowls
- Plastic molds
- Plastic cookie cutters
- Sturdy cardboard boxes
- Clean, empty two-liter soda bottles
- Empty margarine tubs
- Plastic laundry baskets
- Hats (unembellished)
- Small pocketbooks (no sharp hardware or attached decorations)
- Old TV remotes (batteries removed)
- Old cordless phones (batteries removed)
- Clean rags

Toys for One-Year-Olds
Age: 12–24 months

Your child will probably develop from a crawling, babbling baby to a dexterous, talkative toddler over the course of this year. He's growing at an amazing rate, and the toys he plays with should keep up with that rapid development. Toys for

one-year-olds should encourage physical, intellectual, social, and emotional skills. Although he will still enjoy many
toys from the first year—possibly on a different level as his
skills develop —your toddler is now ready for more sophisticated playthings. One word of caution: Remember that
one-year-olds still tend to put things in their mouths, so
make sure anything you give your child is appropriate for
chewing on.

Ride-on and rocking toys

Look for toys that are stable, close to the ground, and pro-
pelled by foot power (pedals are developmentally inappropriate for one-year-olds). Some rockers can be removed
from their base to become ride-ons when your child is
ready. Ride-ons should be comfortable for your child to sit
astride and should steer easily. Buy four-wheeled models
only—three-wheeled vehicles are too tippy. Older one-
year-olds will also enjoy ride-in toys (again, only foot-
powered for this age). Features like working doors, clicking
keys, dumpers, and electronic sound effects add to the
pretend-play value.

Push and pull toys

Both new walkers and almost walkers love push toys, which
give them support as they learn to balance. Look for sturdy,
well-balanced toys that won't tip easily and won't fly out
from under your child. Other features toddlers enjoy are
popping balls, electronic sounds and lights, and space to cart
around small toys.

   More experienced walkers enjoy pull toys like small wagons and animals and vehicles on a tether. Avoid old wooden
toys, which may have lead paint and overly long strings.

Shape sorters

One-year-olds are ready for simple shape sorters, although
they will probably not be able to deal with more than the
three basic shapes (circle, square, and triangle) until they
near their second birthday. Look for shape sorters with big,

chunky shapes that are easy both to put in and to take out (opening some shape sorters is challenging even for adults). Shape sorters teach early spatial-relations skills, manual dexterity, and, in some cases, colors, too. Wooden puzzles with large basic shapes will be enjoyed by older one-year-olds, but save other puzzles for next year.

Manipulatives

Turning, twisting, pressing, pulling, hammering, stacking, and nesting are all dexterity skills that develop greatly during the second year. There are an endless array of toys that encourage these skills. Some of the best are activity tables, beads-on-wire toys, simple tops, hammering benches (with nonremovable pegs), ball pounders (which also encourage tracking skills), stacking cups, nesting boxes, and peg boards with large pegs.

Blocks

Soft, lightweight blocks are best for young toddlers, who are just getting the idea of stacking and building. Colorful cloth and vinyl blocks are good, as are the biggest, most basic connecting blocks.

Musical toys

One-year-olds continue to enjoy electronic musical toys such as play radios, CD players, and keyboards. They are also ready now for simple rhythm instruments like sturdy plastic maracas, tambourines, drums, xylophones, and rhythm sticks. An easy-to-operate jack-in-the-box is also a perennial favorite.

Creative materials

Although they're not yet ready to paint with a brush or color inside the lines, young toddlers love to scribble with crayons. Look for big, easy-to-handle washable ones if you don't want your house redecorated. A large sheet of paper taped to a table, high chair tray, or the floor is the best coloring surface. Some one-year-olds love to finger paint; others don't like the feel of sticky, slimy hands. Young finger painters enjoy experimenting with nontoxic media like chocolate pudding and shaving cream as well as traditional finger paints.

Dolls and puppets

One-year-olds are just beginning to develop the intellectual capacity for pretend play. During this year, their pretending is largely imitative, so they will love a baby doll to rock, a stuffed animal to "feed," or a simple dollhouse to arrange. Look for simple baby dolls with no loose parts (bald heads are preferable) and no dangerous ornamentation on their clothes. Don't bother providing your child with different outfits for his dolls, because it will be years until he has the manual dexterity to use them. Both cloth dolls and small plastic dolls are appropriate for this age. Young toddlers also enjoy puppets, although it will be you who puts on the show for a while yet. Puppets should be made of sturdily sewn cloth with no loose or removable pieces. No marionettes at this age.

Playsets

Another excellent category of toys for toddlers are simple pretend settings like houses, farms, playgrounds, garages, and schools. These self-contained, portable playsets come with big, chunky plastic people, animals, and vehicles that can be enjoyed with or without the setting. Many of these toys are also manipulatives, with handles to crank, wheels to spin, and ramps to maneuver.

Toys for Two-Year-Olds
Age: 21 months–3 years

By the age of two, toddlers have turned into small people who do an amazing job mimicking the lives of the adults around them. They want to talk on the phone, sweep the floor, diaper the baby, and build at a workbench just like you. Two-year-olds also have much more manual dexterity than they did a year ago, and their large-muscle development has turned them into efficient running, jumping, and climbing machines. They will still enjoy many of the same toys they did at one, but they are now ready for some more complex playthings, too—most notably puzzles, creative materials, and pretend play. Here's what you should add at two.

Blocks

Twos continue to enjoy the interlocking blocks they played with last year, but you might want to expand your set now that your child can build more elaborate constructions. Another must-have for this age is a set of big cardboard "bricks" that are strong enough to stack, knock down, and stand on. Some children are ready for a set of wooden blocks at two. If your child throws the blocks or hits with them, put them away and try again in a month or two.

Puzzles

Most two-year-olds aren't ready for jigsaw puzzles, but they will enjoy wooden, plastic, or cardboard puzzles with pieces that fit into their own spaces. Look for sturdy puzzles with pegs on the pieces for easy handling. Some children also enjoy alphabet or number puzzles, but don't push these on a child who's not yet interested in ABCs or 123s.

Dolls

Two-year-olds (and some older one-year-olds) love to play with the characters they know from books and TV. The market is filled with talking, giggling, guitar-playing, vibrating, and flip-flopping versions of these toys, but there's nothing wrong with choosing one without batteries for limitless pretending.

Vehicles

Older toddlers are ready for more detailed vehicles, and many children fall deeply in love with cars, trucks, boats, planes, and trains when they're two. Look for sturdy plastic or wooden vehicles that roll easily and have working parts—trucks that

HOMEMADE PLAY DOUGH RECIPE

Most two-year-olds love to sink their hands (and some-times their teeth) into a big lump of dough. Let them play without accessories at this age—they're still not coordinated enough to handle molds, knives, or cookie cutters. Dough should be used with supervision, because although it's nontoxic, it's not meant to be eaten. Your child will enjoy helping to make his own play dough. Here's the recipe.

1 cup flour
⅓ cup salt
Few drops vegetable oil
Water
Food coloring (optional)

Mix the flour, salt, and vegetable oil together, then add water until the dough is the right consistency (soft but not wet). A few drops of food coloring can be added. Store in a covered container.

load and dump are especially great for the sandbox. Kids love trucks that dump, tow trucks that crank, ladders that raise, trains that they can separate and rearrange, working doors, ramps, horns, and lights. Some two-year-olds are ready to handle simple remote-control vehicles, but make sure you choose one that's meant for this age group. Some two-year-olds are also interested in train sets with tracks. Make sure you get one with no small parts that could be choked on, and realize that you are going to be the one arranging the track for a while yet.

Props for housekeeping
Two is the age kids (both boys and girls) start playing house, and they can never have enough props to use in this creative, role-playing time. Look for telephones, small brooms and

dustpans, vacuums, large plastic tea sets (no china, please), cooking sets, large plastic fake food (make sure nothing is small enough to choke on—kids will put fake food in their mouths), and sturdy doll furniture. Shopping carts and cash registers are great for playing store.

Another great investment for this age—if you have the space—is a play kitchen. Both girls and boys will enjoy this toy for years. Basic models come with a stove, sink, and re-frigerator. More deluxe versions may include a microwave, washing machine, ironing board, built-in table or doll high chair, or even a coffee maker. Look for a kitchen with gender-neutral colors (this is the trend lately). Cooking never looked so easy!

Art supplies

Lots of paper and fat crayons (washable is still your best bet) are the mainstay of a two-year-old's art studio. This year you can also add play dough (bought or made at home, *see recipe on page 169*), washable markers, and tempera paint. Although it's fine to paint at a table, you may want to buy an easel. Look for one with adjustable height and a wide tray for paint cups. Toddlers should use big brushes and only one or two colors at a time. Paint should be nontoxic and wash-able. Surprisingly, some paints being marketed for children are not washable, so be sure to read the label carefully.

Table and chair sets

While not essential, a child-sized table and chair set will be used for years of art projects, snacks, and tea parties. Whether you choose a plastic or a wooden set, make sure it's sturdy and has a top that will stand up to abuse by crayons, play dough, and apple juice. Don't get a set that's too small, because your child will probably use it until he's six or seven.

Books and Multi-Media

Books

It's never too early to introduce your baby to books, and you can never have too many good ones. Reading to your child daily from an early age will not only foster language and cognitive skills, but will also help to form a bond between you that develops from spending special story times together.

Not every children's book out there is worth having on your child's shelf. Look for books with clear, eye-pleasing illustrations (or photographs), age-appropriate stories, and themes that mesh with your views. And don't be discouraged if your three-month-old cries when you read to him, your 10-month-old tosses the book across the room, or your 18-month-old can't sit still until the end of a story. Keep trying. Just a few minutes a day is all it takes to get babies in the habit of looking and listening.

Following are suggestions for wonderful old and new books to help you begin to build a collection of quality children's books for your child.

Books for Babies and Young Toddlers

It is the rare baby under 18 months or so who has the attention span for anything but the shortest, simplest stories. Books for this age group should focus on familiar people and things. Books about animals, household objects, babies, and children, and books about rituals like bathtime and bedtime, are perennial favorites. Very simple stories centered on the events of a baby's day begin to be appreciated from around 12 to 15 months. Sturdy board books are best for babies this age, but don't assume that all board books are appropriate for babies and young toddlers.

Here's a baby top 20:
- *Babies* by Gyo Fujikawa
- *Baby Farm Animals* by Garth Williams

- *Big Red Barn* by Margaret Wise Brown
- *Brown Bear, Brown Bear, What Do You See?* (also *Polar Bear, Polar Bear, What Do You Hear?*) by Eric Carle and Bill Martin, Jr.
- *Color Zoo* (also *Color Farm*) by Lois Ehlert
- *Good Night, Gorilla* by Peggy Rathmann
- *Goodnight Moon* by Margaret Wise Brown and Clement Hurd
- *Hide-and-Seek Elmer* by David McKee
- *Jack: It's Bedtime* (also *Jack: It's Bathtime*; and *Jack: Happy Birthday*) by Rebecca Elgar
- *"More More More," Said the Baby* by Vera B. Williams
- *My First Word Board Book* by Angela Wilkes (also *My First Animal Board Book* by Kenneth Lilly and Deni Brown, and *My First Truck Board Book* by Constance Robinson)
- *My Very First Mother Goose* by Iona Archibald Opie and Rosemary Wells (also individual rhymes published as board books)
- *Old MacDonald* (also *The Itsy Bitsy Spider*) by Rosemary Wells
- *Pat the Bunny* by Dorothy Kunhardt
- *Richard Scarry Early Words* by Richard Scarry
- *Smile!* by Roberta Grobel Intrater
- *Ten, Nine, Eight* by Molly Bang
- *Where's Spot?* (also *Spot's Toy Box*) by Eric Hill

Books for Older Toddlers

As toddlers move into the second half of their second year, their level of comprehension increases dramatically. Even if they're not talking much yet, they can understand everything you say and their attention span is increasing. Now they are ready for books with short, simple stories, although they continue to enjoy their old books. Toddlers still love books about familiar things, other children, and animals. They now also appreciate books with repetitive language, rhyme, and rhythm. And now is the time to begin introducing high-quality alphabet and counting books.

Don't be surprised if your two-year-old begins memorizing his books, and asks for the same books over and over again.

The toddler top 20:

- *Are You My Mother?* by P. D. Eastman
- *Boats* (also *Planes, Trains,* and *Trucks*) by Byron Barton
- *Chicka Chicka Boom Boom* by John Archambault, Lois Ehlert, and Bill Martin, Jr.
- *Corduroy* by Don Freeman
- *Feathers for Lunch* by Lois Ehlert
- *Freight Train* by Donald Crews
- *Green Eggs and Ham* (also *The Foot Book*, *Hop on Pop*, *Dr. Seuss's ABC*, or any of the Dr. Seuss Beginner Books) by Dr. Seuss
- *Harry the Dirty Dog* by Gene Zion
- *How Many Bugs in a Box?* (also *More Bugs in Boxes*, and *Alpha Bugs*) by David A. Carter
- *If You Give a Mouse a Cookie* by Felicia Bond and Laura J. Numeroff
- *Jesse Bear, What Will You Wear?* by Nancy White Carlstrom and Bruce Degen
- *Max's New Suit* (also other Max books) by Rosemary Wells
- *Moo, Baa, La La La!* by Sandra Boynton
- *The Napping House* by Audrey Wood
- *The New Baby* by Fred Rogers
- *Over in the Meadow* by Olive A. Wadsworth and Ezra Jack Keats
- *Peek-a-Boo!* by Janet and Allan Ahlberg
- *Peter's Chair* by Ezra Jack Keats
- *The Runaway Bunny* by Margaret Wise Brown and Clement Hurd
- *The Very Hungry Caterpillar* (also *The Very Busy Spider*, *The Very Quiet Cricket*, and *The Very Lonely Firefly*) by Eric Carle

Videos
Age: 12 months–3 years

Although small children (all children for that matter) should not spend the better part of their day in front of the TV, watching a limited number of well-chosen videos provides both educational enrichment and fun for toddlers over a year old—the age at which most children are first able to attend to the screen for more than a few moments and actually comprehend and become involved in what they are watching.

When you decide to introduce television to your child, it's good to start with videos because you can select exactly what your baby watches and also because toddlers tend to enjoy most shows they have seen before. Although the temptation may be great, don't plunk your child down in front of the TV to watch alone. Sit with him, comment on the characters and action, and be available to answer his questions. The very best videos for toddlers are ones that invite him to get in on the action by dancing, singing, or playing along.

Here are some of the best videos for the very young:

- *Barney's Colors and Shapes* (also *Barney Live in New York City*; all Barney videos are appropriate for this age, but some are better than others)
- *Blue's Clues: Story Time* (also *ABC's and 123's*, *Blue's Birthday*, *Rhythm and Blue*, and *Arts and Crafts*)
- *Elmo's Sing-Along Guessing Game* (also *Get Up and Dance*, and *Learning About Letters*; all Sesame Street videos are appropriate for this age)
- *Here Come the Teletubbies*
- *Kidsongs: Ride the Roller Coaster* (other titles in this series are appropriate for this age, but the quality is uneven)
- *Sweet Dreams, Spot* (also *Where's Spot?*, *Spot Goes to School*, *Spot Goes to a Party*, *Spot Goes to the Farm*)

```
┌─────────────────────────────────────────────────────────┐
│  ⚠        PARENTS ALERT         ⚠                         │
│                                                           │
│  Disney feature films: As well loved as these classic    │
│  films are, they are not appropriate for children under   │
│  three. They're just too scary (and also hard to sit      │
│  through and understand). Save these for later when your  │
│  child will be more able to follow a complicated story    │
│  and separate make-believe from reality.                  │
└─────────────────────────────────────────────────────────┘
```

- *There Goes a Train* (also *Truck*, *Airplane*, *Dump Truck*, *Fire Truck*, *Race Car*)
- *Thomas the Tank Engine* (series)
- *Winnie the Pooh and the Blustery Day* (also *Winnie the Pooh and the Honey Tree*, and *Winnie the Pooh and Tigger Too*; these are the classic Pooh stories, the newer titles are uneven in quality, and some have violent themes, so be sure to preview them before showing them to your child)

Music
Age: Birth and up
From the moment they're born—even, many people believe, before they're born—babies are calmed and soothed by music. As your baby grows, he will go from enjoying gentle lullabies and classical music to responding to a range of music from folk songs to show tunes to jazz to rock. Although you can—and should—share the music you enjoy with your baby, he will also like listening to music that's just for kids. And believe it or not, if you choose wisely, you just might enjoy it, too!

Lullabies
- *A Child's Celebration of Lullaby*
- *All Through the Night*, Mae Robertson, Don Jackson
- *At Quiet O'Clock*, Sally Rogers

⚠ **PARENTS ALERT** ⚠

Loud music: Loud music (above the level of a normal speaking voice) can seriously and permanently harm your child's hearing, so keep the volume down! Babies and toddlers should not listen to music with headphones and should not be allowed to control the volume on the stereo.

- *40 Winks*, Jessica Harper
- *The Planet Sleeps*

Classical Music
- *Bernstein Favorites: Children's Classics*
- *Classics for Kids*
- *Kids Classics Animals* (also *Nature*, *Toys*, and *Lullabies*)
- *The Mozart Effect: Music for Children*, Volumes 1–3

Kiddie Favorites
- *Baby Beluga*, Raffi (or anything by Raffi, including *Singable Songs for the Very Young*, *Rise and Shine*, *One Light One Sun*, and *Raffi in Concert*)
- *Elmopalooza*
- *This Pretty Planet*, Tom Chapin

Folk Music
- *A Child's Celebration of Folk Music*
- *Children's Songs of Woody Guthrie*, Wally Whyton
- *Children's Concert at Town Hall*, Pete Seeger
- *Peter, Paul & Mommy, Too*, Peter, Paul and Mary

Show Tunes and Soundtracks
- *A Child's Celebration of Showtunes*
- *The Lion King: Original Broadway Cast Recording*
- *Classic Disney: 60 Years of Music and Magic*

Computer Software
Age: 2–3 years

For the same reason that children under two shouldn't be allowed to zone out in front of the TV, they shouldn't be plugged into a computer. Babies and young toddlers need to make social contacts and explore their world.

Some two-year-olds are ready to attend to a computer program for a short period of time, and also to start learning how to control a mouse. Your child will need a lot of help at first. You may want to try a mouse made especially for toddlers—it will be easier for him to learn how to use, though it will necessitate the transition to a regular mouse somewhere down the road.

The following software titles are some of the best around for the toddler set. Your child will enjoy sharing these programs with you and learning as he goes.

- *Green Eggs and Ham* or *The Cat in the Hat* (The Learning Company)
- *I Spy Junior* (Scholastic)
- *JumpStart Baby* (Knowledge Adventure)
- *JumpStart Toddlers* (Knowledge Adventure)
- *Just Grandma and Me* (The Learning Company)
- *Richard Scarry's Busytown* (Macmillan)
- *Sesame Street Baby and Me* (The Learning Company)

Chapter 7

Outdoor Safety and Fun

There's no place healthier or more fun for your child than the great outdoors. Every season brings new opportunities to look, listen, run, climb, dig, splash, and explore. But the sun, the water, the grass, and the trees (and all the things that live in them) pose their own set of dangers, too. It's important to be sure that your baby is as well protected outdoors as she is inside your house, which requires making some modifications to your yard and pool. Babies and children are especially vulnerable to hazardous ultraviolet (UV) rays, so scrupulous sunscreen use is in order. Outdoor toys also tend to require more supervision and maintenance than their indoor counterparts because they involve inherent dangers like heights and water. So shop extra carefully to maximize your baby's outdoor safety and fun.

Outdoor Babyproofing

Age: 6 months and up

Although your child will not be playing outdoors without supervision until she is well past her third birthday, it's important to thoroughly childproof your yard just as you would
your house. The best place to start is by fencing all or part of
your yard so that there is no way your child can make her
way into the street. A fully enclosed and gated deck is also a
nice play space for a young child.

Make sure that the space you designate as the play area is
kept clear of debris and in good repair. Install childproof
locks on all gates, and make sure fences are too high to scale
(and too low to crawl under). The following products are
particularly handy for outdoor use.

Bassinet/bouncer with full sun canopy

This is a great place for a very young baby to rest outside. Its
cover zips shut to provide protection from the sun and insects. *(See pages 150–51 for more detail.)*

Portable crib/play yard

If you're planning to use your play yard outdoors, be sure to
get one with a sun canopy and mosquito netting. *(See pages
114–15 and 154–56 for more detail.)*

Large corral-type play yard

The large play area created by this type of gate is perfect for
outdoor fun—you can even put small ride-on or climbing
toys inside. You may want to cover the ground with a plastic
drop cloth if your baby isn't walking yet. *(See pages 154–56
for more detail.)*

Netting for deck railings

If the rails of your deck or balcony are more than 3.5 inches
apart, have them replaced. In the meantime, you can attach

plastic netting in front of the rails to discourage children from trying to squeeze themselves, or anything else, through the openings.

Driveway gate

This freestanding gate does not actually contain children, but rather acts as a deterrent. When placed at the end of a driveway, the gate reminds children not to go into the street and prevents cars from entering the driveway. A long ladder laid across the end of the driveway can serve the same purpose.

Warning signs

You can buy a yellow plastic "Children at Play" sign to place in your driveway to deter traffic. These give some parents a sense of security; others prefer not to call attention to their children's play area.

Sun Protection

Umbrellas and Cabanas
Age: Birth and up

If you're bringing your baby to the beach, it's a good idea to bring some sort of shade with you. A regular beach umbrella is fine as long as the baby stays underneath it. Some parents prefer to place pre-mobile infants into a pop-up cabana or tent. These nylon-and-mesh structures fold down small for easy portability and pop up to form a safe, shady place for a baby to rest and play in. Some have built-in floors; others stake directly into the sand or ground.

Sun-Protective Clothing
Age: 6 months and up

Did you know that a white cotton T-shirt has an SPF of only 5, and that when it gets wet, the SPF drops to almost nothing? While any clothing provides some protection from damaging UV rays, it's unwise to depend on a light T-shirt for full protection from the midday summer sun. If your child is going to be spending long summer days at the beach, you might want to invest in some clothing made especially to protect against UV rays. These light nylon wetsuits, T-shirts, shorts, jackets, and hats block up to 97% of the sun's harmful rays. They are available through specialty Web sites such as The Right Start (www.rightstart.com), Solartex (www.solartex.com), or Sun Grubbies (www.sungrubbies.com).

Sunscreen
Age: Birth and up

It's now common knowledge that most of the sun damage that leads to skin cancer and premature aging occurs during childhood. That, along with the obvious sensitivity of your baby's tender skin, is why it's absolutely crucial to protect your baby from the sun. The best thing you can do is to keep your baby completely out of direct sunlight (especially for the first six months). The next best thing is sunscreen. Although it was long believed that infants under six months old should not wear sunscreen, new research has shown that you can and should use sunscreen on babies from birth (look for an SPF of at least 15, preferably 30).

⚠️   **PARENTS ALERT**   ⚠️

Sunscreens: No matter what the label says, all sunscreens eventually wash off when your baby gets wet. To make sure that your baby is protected from the sun at all times, reapply her sunscreen following every swimming session.

ALL ABOUT SUNSCREEN

Your baby should wear sunscreen whenever she is exposed to direct sunlight for more than a few minutes, especially in summer or in southern climates—not just on the beach, but in the park, in the stroller, and in the snow. If your baby has fair skin, she should wear a sunscreen with an SPF of at least 30. If she has dark skin, an SPF of at least 15 should be enough in most cases. The sunscreen should block out both UVB (short) and UVA (long) ultraviolet rays (most brands do). You should also make sure that the sunscreen contains neither PABA, which may irritate the skin, nor fragrances or color, so read the label carefully.

Before applying sunscreen to your child for the first time, test it to make sure that she doesn't have an allergic reaction. Apply a bit of the sunscreen to the inside of her arm and put a bandage over it for 24 hours. Then expose the spot to the sun for a few minutes. If the area reddens, swells, itches, or reacts in any way, try a different product. If any sunscreen produces an adverse reaction at any time, discontinue its use immediately. Also, be sure to keep sunscreen out of your baby's eyes and off her hands (which will often be in her mouth).

Apply sunscreen to your baby at least 15 minutes before you go outside so it can be thoroughly absorbed for maximum protection. Reapply every two hours or every time your baby comes out of the water. And remember that even the most vigilant sunscreen regimen does not protect your baby completely. It's still wise to avoid long exposure to the strong midday sun.

Once a baby passes the six-month mark, she should wear a children's sunscreen, also PABA-free with an SPF of at least 15 (most sunscreens marketed for children have an SPF of 30 to 40) whenever she's in the sun. Babies should also wear sun hats with wide brims to protect their heads and faces. Colored zinc oxide sticks are useful for protecting especially vulnerable areas such as noses, cheeks, and shoulders.

Sunglasses
Age: Birth and up
Some doctors recommend putting sunglasses on tiny infants if they're going to be out in the glaring sun—but tiny infants should never be out in the glaring sun. Sunglasses are fine for babies over a year old, as long as they are willing to wear them—many aren't. SoftShades™ sunglasses, held on by soft foam and a cloth headband, are appropriate for children 6 months and older. Make sure they fit well and have plastic lenses and a sticker that says they block 100 percent of UV rays.

Pool Safety

Having a swimming pool in your back yard is great fun, but it can also pose extreme danger for your child. Drowning is the third most common cause of accidental death for children, and it can happen more quickly than you ever thought possible. If you have a pool, every adult in your household should be trained in cardiopulmonary resuscitation (CPR). Hundreds of children are saved from drowning every year with CPR. CPR courses are taught by the Red Cross nationwide, and also through many YMCAs, community centers, hospitals, and pediatricians' offices. Ask your child's doctor for a recommendation.

Closely supervise your child at all times near the pool, and never leave your child near a pool without an adult who can swim. All pools should also be fenced within the yard.

Even if your yard is fenced, you must have a barrier between the play area and the pool. The fence should be at least four feet high with rails or slats not more than 3.5 inches apart, and no handholds or footholds that would make it possible for it to be climbed over. The fence should have a self-closing, self-latching gate with a childproof lock at least four and a half feet from the ground, and the pool deck should be made of nonslip material. Remove ladders that enable easy access to the water of an aboveground pool. And always drain wading pools when not in use.

Don't go in the water with an infant who cannot yet hold her head upright on her own—around four or five months of age. Make sure the water temperature is at least 84 degrees Fahrenheit for infants under six months, and at least 74 degrees Fahrenheit for older babies and toddlers. Kids should come out of the water after about half an hour, or sooner if they show signs of being cold.

The water should be kept clean and chemically balanced at all times. You should not allow children to drink pool water; untreated water could contain microbes that could make your baby sick, and the chemicals in treated water could also harm your child. Anything mechanical, including pumps and filters, should be kept in good working order.

Rescue equipment at poolside should include a long pole with a crook at the end, at least one ring-shaped life preserver, and a long rope. There should also be a rope with buoys separating the deep from the shallow water. Always have a portable phone poolside to save precious seconds in case of an emergency.

When you close your pool for the winter, cover it with an approved cover that complies with ASTM (American Society for Testing and Materials) standards and supports at least thirty pounds per square foot. Make sure it is securely fastened, and never assume that a covered pool is safe. Many drownings occur when children slip between the cover and the side of the pool.

Pool Alarms

Although no alarm is foolproof and nothing replaces constant supervision, a pool alarm can add another barrier between your child and the water. There are several different types of alarms to consider.

Door-exit alarm

Any door or accessible window that leads directly to a pool should be equipped with an alarm. It's important to keep the alarm activated at all times when your child may be moving about the house.

Fence-gate alarm

Installing an alarm on your fence gate adds an extra measure of protection by alerting you if your child (or anyone else's) enters the pool area.

Infrared motion detector

Like those used in home-security systems, infrared motion detectors can be placed around a pool area to be activated by any motion on the pool deck.

 PARENTS ALERT

Bowel movements in the pool: Always dress babies and toddlers in swim diapers to prevent leakage of bowel movements. But remember that such diapers do not completely prevent the dispersal of fecal bacteria. If any child has a bowel movement in the pool, have everyone leave the pool immediately and replace and treat the water appropriately to prevent infection with *E. coli,* a bacterium that can be life-threatening in small children.

In-pool motion detector

This type of motion detector sounds an alarm if there is sudden motion in the water. False alarms may occur, however, if animals or debris fall into the pool.

Clip-on alarm

This alarm clips onto a child's clothing (some are bracelet style) and activate when they get wet. False alarms may occur during hand washing or similar wet activities. There is also the potential for the alarm to detach from your child without your knowledge.

Flotation Devices
Age: 6 months and up

There are many types of flotation devices for children, from U.S. Coast Guard–approved life jackets that keep the

Bubble and Flotation Swimsuit

head above water even if the wearer is unconscious to inflatable inner tubes that are purely for fun. With the exception of certain types of life jackets, flotation devices are not designed to keep a child's head above water. Although they can help keep a child afloat when they're in working condition, they should not be relied upon to keep your child safe and should be used only under strict supervision. Flotation devices can lead to a false sense of security for both parent and child, so be aware and vigilant at all times.

These are the basic types of flotation devices for infants and toddlers.

Life jacket

Life jackets are mostly used on boats, although some toddlers use them for extra buoyancy in the pool. A Coast Guard–approved life jacket is the best flotation device, though it is not very comfortable to wear. Type II personal flotation devices are designed to keep an unconscious wearer face up in the water. This type of nylon life vest zips up the front and has a large buoyant flap hanging behind the neck, which makes it awkward for casual use in the pool. Type III life jackets are made to keep the wearer in a vertical or slightly backward-tilted position in the water. They have flotation panels in the back and the chest of the vest, and are more comfortable than type II. All life jackets should fit properly (size is according to weight) for maximum protection.

          PARENTS ALERT

Stomachaches: Never let a child swim within a week of a bout of diarrhea or other gastrointestinal disease.

Bubble

A bubble is a buoyant device that clips around a child's torso. It could have buoyant pads only in the back or in both the front and the back. While the bubble helps keep the child afloat, she must know how to move her arms and legs in a paddling motion to keep her face out of the water. Bubbles are appropriate for children over 18 months old who are beginning to learn how to swim.

Flotation swimsuit

These are basically swimsuits with a built-in bubble or inner tube. Unless it is specifically labeled as a Coast Guard–approved flotation device, you cannot depend on such a suit to keep your child afloat; it is simply a flotation aid.

Water wings

Water wings are inflatable cuffs that are worn around the top of a child's arms to increase buoyancy. A child must be able to dog paddle to make use of water wings, as they will not keep an unmoving child afloat. Suitable for children two and older.

Floats and tubes

There are many kinds of inflatable floats, tubes, and balls that should be considered pool toys rather than flotation devices. Although they will keep a child afloat if properly inflated, such toys puncture easily and must be completely inflated for maximum buoyancy. One type of float has a seat (much like that in a walker or stationary exerciser) that a baby under 25 pounds sits in, enabling her to float and kick around in the water. Some babies enjoy this immensely, but they must be supervised at all times.

Play Equipment

Foot-Powered Ride-Ons
Age: 12 months–3 years

Ride-on toys that toddlers can sit astride and move with their feet are great for both indoors and out—look for slightly larger and sturdier models for outdoor play. Ride-on toys should be well balanced and easy for a small child to mount and dismount. Four wheels are best for stability, and the front two should steer easily. Although wooden toys are classic looking, plastic holds up better for outdoor use.

Ride-In Vehicles
Age: 12 months and up

These foot-powered vehicles look like something out of *The Flintstones.* Available in models from cars to trucks to jeeps to tractors, these plastic fantasy-mobiles are loved by toddlers of both sexes. Much of the allure of these vehicles comes from the fact that you can open the door, get inside, and close it behind you. From that point, children go in several different directions. Some simply sit in the car, grasp the steering wheel, and make motor noises. Others put two feet on the floor and tool around. Still others tinker with the clicking key or other moving parts. Whatever type of driver you have, this will be one of the best-loved toys of your child's preschool years. Don't be tempted to get a pedal or battery-powered vehicle—both are developmentally inappropriate for children under three.

Wagons

Wagons come in all shapes and sizes. Some are made to be pulled by a child, others for a child or children to sit in and be pulled by an adult. Although metal and wooden wagons are classics and are great for hauling gear, the newer plastic models are much better for human passengers. Look for a sturdy plastic wagon with seats so that two children can ride facing each other. Many have a door for easy entry and exit, and a cup holder for snacks on the road.

Tricycles
Age: 2 years and up

Although many children don't learn to pedal and steer until after their third birthday, there are some who can handle small tricycles as early as two years. If you're buying for a toddler, look for a small trike that your child can get onto and off of without assistance. Trikes should be stable and low to the ground, and have tires with treads so the wheels don't slip. A high seat back is another nice feature for this age. Trikes with detachable push bars are back savers for parents teaching little ones how to ride.

Helmet

Although it is not a necessity for a tricycle rider, it can't hurt for your child to wear a helmet. And wearing one now will get her into the habit. Look for a toddler-sized helmet with plenty of ventilation and comfortable padding.

Sandboxes
Age: 18 months and up

Kids love to play in the sand, and sand play is great for exploring textures and filling and pouring experiments. Look

PARENTS ALERT

Asbestos in play sand: Some limestone-based sand marketed as play sand for sandboxes contains a form of asbestos called tremolite. Although CPSC does not consider tremolite to be dangerous at the levels at which it is present in play sand, you may want instead to purchase sand that is silica based, like beach sand.

for a smooth plastic sandbox with sturdy sides. A box big enough for more than one or two children to play in is a plus as kids grow older. The most important feature to look for in a sandbox is a watertight cover. Be sure to replace the cover after every play session to keep out yard debris, as well as animals and the things they leave behind.

Sand toys

Buckets and shovels should be smooth plastic without any sharp or rough edges. Metal sand toys, no matter how beautiful, are a trip to the plastic surgeon waiting to happen. Buckets, shovels, rakes, sieves, funnels, and simple sand mills are appropriate for toddlers. Save fancy molds for later—they will frustrate one- and two-year-olds, who don't have the coordination to use them.

Climbing Toys
Age: 12 months–3 years

Small-scale climbing toys and slides are great fun for toddlers. Look for sturdy and smooth plastic construction with plenty of closely spaced handholds. Slides should slope

---

 PARENTS ALERT

Pressure-treated wood: In 1990, a study released by the Consumer Product Safety Commission raised concerns about the safety of wood that was treated with chromated copper arsenic as a preservative. In 1998, however, the CPSC concluded that this wood was safe for playground use as it does not contain enough dangerous chemicals to be harmful. If you want a wooden swing set and wish to avoid pressure-treated wood, look for one made of (much pricier) naturally insect-resistant cedar or redwood.

INSTALLING PLAY EQUIPMENT

For safety's sake, it's important that all play equipment be assembled and installed properly. Unless you are very handy and scrupulous in following directions, consider hiring a professional to assemble your swing set. It's imperative that instructions are followed to the letter to ensure that the set will be safe.

Equipment should be installed on a soft surface, such as sand or wood chips, that is 6 to 12 inches deep and extends at least 6 feet on all sides of the equipment. Grass is not considered a safe surface because it can wear down, and the ground can get hard-packed. The set should be placed at least 6 feet from fences, buildings, trees, or anything else that could get in the way and create a hazard.

Metal swing sets must be anchored into the ground with concrete footings. Make sure these are secure and do not protrude above the ground and cause a tripping hazard. Most wooden play equipment is staked into the ground—make sure the stakes extend deep enough to make the set motionless and secure.

Finally, make frequent safety checks to make sure nuts and bolts remain tight and embedded, wood stays smooth, and all footings are secure. Regular maintenance is necessary to ensure that your play equipment remains safe and fun.

gently for this age. Climbers with built-in playhouses or tunnels provide even more fun.

Gardening Toys
Age: 2 years and up

Toddlers will enjoy puttering in the garden alongside Mom or Dad. Although kid-sized trowels, hoes, and rakes are available in authentic wood and metal versions, these are not the best idea for toddlers, as they can splinter, rust, and cause major injuries. Look for smooth plastic shovels, hoes, rakes, watering cans, wheelbarrows, and pretend lawn mowers. But children should never be outside when a real lawn mower is being used.

Swing Sets
Age: 2 years and up

Although babies enjoy swinging in a high-backed baby swing from about the age of six months, they won't be able to do much of anything else with a swing set until they are around two and a half, so hold off on this major purchase until your first child is at least that age. Depending on your space, taste, and budget, swing sets can be simple or spectacular, but every swing set must be safe. Whether you buy a basic metal set from a toymart or a custom wooden playscape from a private dealer, every set must be installed and maintained properly. And it goes without saying that children, especially toddlers, should be closely supervised any time they're on or near the equipment. Be sure to buy from a place where you can see the equipment set up.

Here's what to look for:
- Sturdy construction.
- Smooth materials—wood that won't splinter, or metal without any sharp edges.
- Swings hung on nylon ropes rather than chains (which can pinch little fingers and be hard to grip). If swings are hung on chains, the chains should be covered by vinyl sleeves.
- Soft swings (like a strap) that conform to the child's body. These are safer, easier to get onto and off of, and don't cause as much damage if they hit somebody.
- Baby swings with high backs and secure straps, including a crotch strap, or one-piece construction with holes for the legs.

- Spaces of at least 9—but no more than 12—inches between ladder rungs and between the ladder and the platform, so a child's head can't get caught.
- The bottom of the slide less than one foot off the ground.
- Nuts and bolts that are embedded so they can't snag skin or clothing.
- Platforms with guardrails.

Sleds
Age: 12 months and up
Sleds are great fun for children who can sit steadily and hold on. Look for a sled specifically made for babies and toddlers. It should have wide, smooth runners; high sides and a backrest; and a secure safety belt. The sled should also have a strong tow rope, which an adult should hold at all times and use to pull the sled around on flat ground. Never send a young child coasting down a hill.

Snow Toys
Age: 18 months and up
Let your little helper give you a hand clearing the sidewalk with her own mini plastic snow shovel. Sand shovels and pails are also fun in the snow.

Snow art (2–3 years)
Add food coloring to water in a squirt bottle, and you have snow paint! These are also available commercially.

Wading Pools
Age: 6 months and up
Babies and toddlers love to cool off in a wading pool on a hot summer day; but, as in the bath, they must be supervised at all times. The best kiddie pools are hard plastic with sturdy sides. These are the easiest to dry, drain (make sure it has a drain plug), and clean. They are also much easier for cruisers to pull up on and toddlers to climb into and out of than inflatable or soft-sided vinyl pools. Added features like gentle sprinklers or small slides make kiddie pools even more fun.

Sprinklers
Age: 18 months and up

Gentle sprinklers are wonderful for toddlers. Look for one that doesn't spray too high or too hard (many made for older children are quite powerful). Often young children actually prefer a sprinkler to a wading pool, but if your child seems overwhelmed or frightened by the spray, put it away for a few weeks and try again.

Chapter 8

Gift-Giving Guide

Giving gifts to babies can be a tricky business. You must consider sizes and seasons, developmental levels and temperament, and—often most important—what the child (or the parents-to-be) already has. There are several easy ways out of this dilemma. Money gifts—in the form of cash, bonds, or other financial products—are an investment in the baby's future. Savings or treasury bonds are popular because they can be purchased in relatively small increments and are a secure investment that will grow over time. Gift certificates are also great, because they don't take much time and effort to buy, and they assure that the new parents will receive a gift they really want—and that the money will go toward a gift for the baby (not always the case with cash gifts). Another option is to buy from a gift registry. You won't find many two-year-olds who register for birthday gifts (yet), but more and more expectant mothers are registering for shower gifts at large baby chain stores. You also could ask

BABY GIFTS FOR MOM AND DAD

Let's face it, a newborn baby is completely unaware of any gift he's receiving, so you're really buying to please his parents. And while all the traditional baby gifts are certainly appreciated, some of the most thoughtful and cherished gifts can't be bought at the baby superstore or the mall. Having a baby is an upheaval is any couple's (or family's) life, and one of the best gifts in this hectic period is a gift of help and time. Here are some ideas for how to give both creatively:

- *Baby-sitting.* The best of all possible gifts, but one that new parents often find it hard to ask for (or, sometimes, take when offered). Don't just offer to baby-sit "sometime"—make plans for a specific day or evening. Call a week in advance and ask the parents if they would like to go out on Saturday night, or tell them that you are available every Wednesday from 2:00 to 5:00. Call them; don't wait for them to call you. The ultimate in baby-sitting is an overnight (if the mother isn't nursing).
- *Household help.* Take housekeeping responsibilities off the shoulders of new parents by hiring a cleaning person or service for several visits, or pitching in and doing it yourself (don't wait to be asked!).
- *Meals.* One or more freezable, easy-to-serve meals will be greatly appreciated, especially during the first month or so. Make them yourself, or order them and have them delivered.
- *Dinner out.* Another good way to give the parents some time alone together is to give them a gift certificate for a favorite restaurant or tickets to a show or game. An offer to baby-sit when they go is not required, but it makes the gift that much better!
- *Relaxation.* Give a gift certificate for a massage or a spa visit (again, an offer to baby-sit sweetens the gift).

BABY GIFTS FOR MOM AND DAD
(continued)

- *Pampering.* Give an exhausted new mother a gift of bubble bath, body lotion, aromatherapy products, or anything else to nurture her.

---

the parents what they want or need—a practical strategy, but one that takes away the fun of a surprise. The last—and best—method for picking out the perfect baby gift is to refer to the lists in this chapter, which were compiled from the responses of many veteran baby-gift receivers.

But first, a few words of baby gift-giving wisdom:

- If you can, wait until you know the sex of the baby before you buy clothing or decorative items.
- Handmade gifts are the most special of all. If you knit, crochet, embroider, sew, quilt, or work with wood, consider making a baby gift. It will be cherished above all others. Make sure all handmade items are safe for a baby.
- Ignore advice to buy clothes in large sizes—most parents appreciate outfits that their baby can wear within the first six months. This way, your gift will always be in style and fit when it's seasonally appropriate.
- Pay attention to the seasons. Don't buy a short romper for an August baby (or the same in a twelve-month size for a June baby)—it will get little or no wear. Instead, opt for a fleece bunting or a warm sleeper in a three- or six-month size.
- Don't buy large pieces of equipment such as strollers, car seats, or high chairs unless you know exactly which model the parents prefer.
- Also, don't buy diaper bags, bottle sets, pacifiers, and breast pumps unless you know exactly which model the parents want. These are very personal items that the parents will want to choose themselves.

- Buy from a place where the recipient can make returns easily. Get gift receipts if possible.

Gifts for Newborns

Choosing a gift for a new baby presents the giver with almost unlimited options, particularly if the recipient is a first child. Clothing is probably the most popular gift because it's so much fun to pick out. If you do decide to give clothing, refer to the advice above *(pages 198–99)*, as well as that in Chapter 2 *(pages 35–56)*, to ensure that what you give is appropriate and useful.

Gifts of baby equipment like furniture, bedding, strollers, carriers, high chairs, infant seats, swings, and portable cribs are greatly appreciated also, as long as you know exactly what the parents want and need. Items like blankets, towels, picture frames, and photo albums are good choices for people you don't know well, because you can never have too many of them.

Another category of gifts that people buying for newborns often overlook is toys, books, and music. Most new parents are thrilled to receive all three, whether the gift can be put to use immediately (an activity arch, crib mirror, cloth book, or lullaby CD) or will be saved for a later stage (Mother Goose book, activity quilt, rattle). One category of toys to avoid is stuffed animals. Although they're cute, the new parents are sure to receive a boatload of them, which will end up collecting dust on a shelf or forgotten in a storage closet. Exceptions are special handmade stuffed toys (check to make sure they are safe for babies) or pull-down musical animals, which babies love from the start.

Here are some ideas, broken down by price category, for buying gifts for a new baby:

Over $100
- Baby nurse or doula (the ultimate gift for those who want it)

- Video camera
- Stroller/car seat system
- Lightweight stroller
- Cashmere baby blanket
- Portable crib/play yard
- Personalized toy box

$50–$100

- Chenille baby blanket
- Hand-knit cotton sweater (cardigans especially)
- Ear thermometer
- Bouncer/bassinet (for a summer baby)
- Soft baby carrier
- Battery-operated baby swing
- Instant camera (Polaroid)
- Baby monitor with two receivers
- Child-sized rocking chair

$25–50

- Soft-floor gym
- Crib mobile
- Hand-knit hat and booties set
- Microfleece baby blanket
- Fleece bunting (for a fall or winter baby)
- Bouncer with vibration, toy bar, and canopy
- Tape or CD player (for the nursery)
- Remote-control crib cassette player
- Activity quilt
- Baby book (scrapbook for recording baby's firsts)
- Silver picture frame
- Photo album
- Baby monitor with one receiver

Under $25

- Cotton baby blanket
- Hooded towel and washcloth set
- Musical pull-down toy
- Books (*see pages 171–73 for suggestions*)

- Music cassettes or CDs (*see pages 175–76 for suggestions*)
- Crib mirror
- Black-and-white infant stimulation toys
- Infant car seat toy bar
- Baby food mill
- Convertible infant/toddler bathtub
- Inflatable baby bathtub
- Bright, lightweight rattles or high chair toys
- Subscription to *Parents* magazine (800-727-3682)

First Birthday Gifts

A baby's first birthday is a huge milestone—especially for his parents! The tiny, helpless bundle they brought home from the hospital a few short months ago is now a crawling, climbing, babbling little person full of energy and fun. Gone from a one-year-old's life are buntings, bouncy seats, baby swings, crib mobiles, and carriers. Now he needs toys to push, pull, stack, roll, and hug. One-year-olds love anything that exercises their bodies or their minds, so this is also a great time to give books and music (*see pages 157–77, for a full guide to buying toys and media*).

Clothing is also a great one-year-old gift, since everything from the preceding year is sure to have been outgrown. Again, pay attention to sizing and seasons, and try to buy for the present or near future rather than months down the road. Particularly appreciated are special items like hand-knit sweaters or smocked dresses that parents tend not to splurge on themselves. Don't hesitate to ask the parents if you're unsure of their child's size, and be sure to get a gift receipt.

Here are some first birthday ideas, by price:

Over $100
- Jogging stroller
- High-quality rocking horse, boat, or airplane

AND BABY MAKES FOUR . . . OR MORE— GIFTS FOR SECOND CHILDREN AND BEYOND

When parents bring home their second, third, or tenth baby, their excitement is just as great as it was for their first, but their need for clothing and equipment is not. By the second time around, most families already have most of the equipment they need, and sometimes many of the clothes. Although something new is always appreciated, there is a certain knack required to pick out just the right gift for experienced parents. Here are some tips:

- Avoid furniture and equipment such as strollers, high chairs, portable cribs, bouncer seats, bathtubs, and the like. Two exceptions to this rule: Something wonderfully innovative that has been introduced since their last child was born, or if the closest sibling is more than four years older.
- A double stroller is a great gift if the older sibling is three or under. Ask the parents which one they prefer.
- Personalized gifts make non-firstborns feel particularly special.
- Monetary gifts will be even more appreciated with two or more to educate.
- If the new baby is a different gender from any of the family's other children, bring on the clothes. The baby will also need a new wardrobe if same-sex siblings were born at different times of year.
- Gifts of help and time will be even more needed with each additional child (see pages 197–98).
- If you're bringing the new baby a gift, it's very nice (although not expected) to bring something small for the siblings as well. If you're a family member, this is a must. If you're sending your gift through the mail, sibling gifts aren't necessary.

$50–$100

- Climbing toy or slide
- Backpack baby carrier
- Plastic wagon
- Large beads-on-wire table
- Ride-on with electronic sounds and lights
- Personalized step stool

$25–50

- Activity table
- Beads-on-wire toy
- Set of rhythm instruments
- Electronic musical toy
- Rocking toy
- Ride-on toy
- Toy farm or garage

Under $25

- Stacking cups
- Stacking rings (not graduated in size)
- Pounding toy
- Simple baby doll
- Toy piano or xylophone
- Books (*see pages 171–73 for suggestions*)
- Music cassettes or CDs (*see pages 175–76 for suggestions*)
- Push or pull toy
- Simple shape sorter
- Fabric blocks
- Connecting blocks
- Soft balls
- Toy phone
- Chunky vehicles

GIVING TO MULTIPLES

Buying gifts for multiples is not as easy as buying a baby gift in duplicate, triplicate, or more. Parents expecting multiple babies need two (or more) of some things, like cribs, car seats, high chairs, and clothing (although many parents of multiples don't want identical outfits). Some parents may want more than one swing, portable crib/play yard, bassinet, baby carrier, or bouncer, while others prefer to rotate their babies through a variety of equipment. If you're close enough to the parents to be buying such large gifts, it's a good idea to ask them exactly what they would like. Here are some ideas for newborn multiples:

- A double or triple stroller will be the most appreciated of all gifts. Just make sure to buy the exact model the parents have picked out.
- If you're buying clothing for same-sex twins, don't get identical outfits (unless you know that's what the parents want). On the other hand, don't buy completely unrelated things, either (a snow suit and a party dress, for example). The same outfit in different colors or the same type of category of clothing (overalls, dresses, sleepers) is the way to go.
- One gift for the multiples is fine, as long as it's something that's for the household rather than for an individual. For example, one ear thermometer is fine, but one baby carrier is not. Try to resist the temptation to spend the same amount on a gift or gifts for all the babies as you would on one. After all, each baby is an individual.
- A must-have book about multiples is *Having Twins and More: A Parent's Guide to Multiple Pregnancy, Birth, and Early Childhood* by Elizabeth Noble and Leo Sorger.

GIVING TO MULTIPLES

- Personalized gifts (rocking chairs, step stools, piggy banks) are especially nice for multiples. A personalized seesaw for a set of twins is one of the cutest gifts ever.

Before the babies are old enough to know the difference, it's fine to give unrelated toys—a floor gym and a set of bath toys, for example. Once the multiples are old enough to compare, however, it's best to stick to two different versions of the same toy—two different puzzles, toy trucks, shape sorters, balls, or pull toys. When buying gifts for older multiples, one for each is always better than one for all. And for toys that will be very close to the child's heart—like dolls or stuffed animals—it's best to give identical items.

One last piece of advice: Once the babies are old enough to open their gifts themselves, put every present, no matter how small, in a separate box, so each child has something to unwrap.

Second Birthday Gifts

Two-year-olds have developed into both thinkers and doers, so they're ready for gifts that exercise their abilities in new and exciting ways. This birthday is the first for which most children understand what's going on, and they absolutely love receiving—and opening—presents. It's also the first year that the young recipient may actually show disappointment if a gift is not what was hoped for. Don't take this personally—two-year-olds don't understand the niceties of showing appreciation, although most can say thank you when prompted.

At two, toddlers are ready for more complicated manipulative toys, larger toys to climb and slide on, and puzzles and books that require more brain power. They also love gifts that stretch their quickly expanding imaginations, like pretend props and art supplies. Great classic gifts for this age are blocks, play dough, easels (along with crayons, paper, and painting supplies), dolls and doll equipment, table and chair sets, puzzles, sand toys, and riding toys.

Clothing is also a great gift, as are books, music, and software. Children this age love videos, but before buying, make sure to talk to the parents about the kinds of things they allow their child to watch.

Here are some ideas for two-year-olds:

Over $100
- Swing set
- Playhouse
- Large climber
- Table for wooden trains
- High-quality table and chair set

⚠ PARENTS ALERT ⚠

Unsafe packaging: For toddlers, the fun of opening a present often outweighs the thrill of the gift itself. This is fine as long as gift opening is closely supervised. Don't let your child play with dangerous items such as plastic bags (which can suffocate), Styrofoam peanuts (which can choke), ribbon (which can strangle), or boxes with staples, twist ties, or other sharp or small objects. The best way to handle present opening for the under-three set is to let them do the unwrapping and then take over from there yourself.

$50–$100
- Ride-in car or truck
- Small tricycle
- Simple plastic or wooden doll house with furniture and doll family
- Puppet theater
- Table and chair set
- Play kitchen
- Play store
- Wooden easel
- Interlocking-block table
- Small plastic seesaw
- Large plastic kiddie pool

$25–$50
- Sandbox
- Wooden train starter set
- Plastic easel
- Electronic learning toy
- Large set of interlocking blocks
- Large set of wooden blocks
- Toy guitar
- Child-sized adjustable basketball hoop
- Pop-up tent or ball pit

Under $25
- Realistic baby doll
- Simple doll furniture or stroller
- Character doll
- Wooden puzzle
- Books *(see pages 171–73 for suggestions)*
- Music cassettes or CDs *(see pages 175–76 for suggestions)*
- Computer software *(see page 177 for suggestions)*
- Videos *(see pages 174–75 for suggestions)*
- Cardboard building bricks
- Bath toys

- Sand toys
- Fire engine or dump truck
- Puppet
- Play dough
- Washable crayons and drawing paper
- Picnic set with toy food
- Plastic tea set
- Toddler sprinkler

Chapter 9

Resources

Product and Safety Information

Environmental Defense Fund
257 Park Avenue South
New York, NY 10010
www.environmentaldefense.org

The Environmental Defense Fund (EDF) is a nonprofit organization devoted to environmental protection. They publish brochures, newsletters, and books on environmental issues, including many relating to consumer protection issues. Their brochure on lead in china (available at www.environmental defense.org/pubs/brochures/LeadInChina or by writing to Lead-Safe China Brochure, Environmental Defense, P.O. Box 96969, Washington, DC 20090) is particularly informative. They also provide a list of low-lead china patterns.

Juvenile Products Manufacturers Association (JPMA)
17000 Commerce Pkwy, Suite C
Mount Laurel, NJ 08054
www.jpma.org

This is a national trade organization for companies that manufacture or import infant products such as furniture, car seats, strollers, bedding, and decorative items (not toys or clothing). The JPMA has a rigorous safety certification program in which manufacturers may voluntarily choose to participate. Products that meet JPMA's standards are given a seal that identifies them as meeting the highest safety standards for purchase and use. The organization also offers a brochure entitled "Safe and Sound for Baby," which describes their certification program and gives information on baby product selection and use. You can download it from their Web site, or send a stamped, self-addressed envelope to the above address for a print copy.

National Highway Traffic Safety Administration
400 Seventh Street, SW
Washington, DC 20590
www.nhtsa.gov

The NHTSA's Web site provides information on child passenger safety, including a car seat inspection station locator. Their auto safety hotline at 888-327-4236 provides safety information on cars, trucks, and related equipment such as car seats.

National Lead Information Center
422 South Clinton Ave.
Rochester, NY 14620
www.epa.gov/lead/nlic.htm

This organization provides information about lead hazards and state and local agencies that can provide testing and other information. Visit their Web site to order documents or call 800-424-5323.

National Radon Hotline
800-SOS-RADON
www.nsc.org/ehc/indoor/hotlines.htm

This hotline provides a recorded message about radon and a basic information packet that includes a coupon for a low-cost radon test kit. To speak to someone directly about radon, call 800-55-RADON or contact your state's radon department,which you can locate at www.epa.gov/iaq/contacts.html.

National Safety Council
1121 Spring Lake Drive
Itasca, IL 60143 .
www.nsc.org

This nonprofit service organization is dedicated to improving the safety, health, and environmental health of all people. The council's Environmental Health Center provides information and community-based programs on environmental and public health issues. Visit their Web site or call 800-621-7619 for information.

Toy Industry Association
200 Fifth Avenue, Suite 740
New York, NY 10010
www.toy-tia.org

This manufacturers' association publishes a guide to selecting age-appropriate toys called "Fun Play, Safe Play." It is available on their Web site, or call 877-486-9723 to order a print copy.

Underwriters Laboratories
333 Pfingsten Road
Northbrook, IL 60062
www.ul.com/consumers/index.html

UL is an organization committed to consumer safety. Visit their Web site for juvenile product safety information. To verify a product's UL listing, call 877-854-3577.

U.S. Consumer Product Safety Commission
Washington, DC 20207
800-638-2772
www.cspc.gov

This is an independent federal regulatory agency charged with protecting the public from risks associated with consumer products. Contact this agency to find out if any product you're using or planning to purchase has been recalled and to report any problems with products you have used.

Juvenile Product Information

Avent
800-542-8368
www.aventamerica.com

Baby Jogger
800-241-1848
www.babyjogger.com

Baby Trend
800-328-7363
www.babytrend.com

Bellini
www.bellini.com

Britax
704-409-1700
www.britaxusa.com

Century
800-837-4044
www.centuryproducts.com

Child Craft
812-883-3111
www.childcraftind.com

Combi
800-992-6624
www.combi-intl.com

Dovel Juvenile Group
800-544-1108
www.djgusa.com

Evenflo
800-233-5921
www.evenflo.com

The First Years
800-317-3194
www.thefirstyears.com

Fisher-Price
800-432-5437
www.fisher-price.com

Gerber
800-443-7237
www.gerber.com

Graco
800-345-4109
www.gracobaby.com

Kolcraft
800-453-7673
www.kolcraft.com

Maclaren
877-442-4622
www.maclarenbaby.com

Medela
800-435-8316
www.medela.com

Morigeau-Lépine
450-462-2111
www.morigeau.com

Nojo
www.nojo.com

Peg-Pérego
800-671-1701
www.perego.com

Playtex
800-222-0453
www.playtexbaby.com

Prince Lionheart
800-544-1132
www.princelionheart.com

Ragazzi
www.ragazzi.com

Safety 1st
800-544-1108
www.safety1st.com

Sassy
616-243-0767
www.sassybaby.com

Simmons
920-982-2140
www.simmonsjp.com

Toy Manufacturers

Crayola
800-272-9652
www.crayola.com

Fisher-Price
800-432-5437
www.fisher-price.com

Hasbro
800-327-8264
www.hasbro.com

Kenner
800-327-8264
www.hasbro.com

Learning Curve
800-704-8697
www.learningcurve.com

Lego
800-453-4652
www.lego.com

Little Tikes
800-321-0183
www.littletikes.com

Mattel
800-524-8697
www.mattel.com

Milton Bradley
888-836-7025
www.hasbro.com

Nerf
800-327-8264
www.hasbro.com

Ohio Art
419-636-7206
www.world-of-toys.com

Parker Brothers
888-836-7025
www.hasbro.com

Playhut
888-PLAYHUT
www.playhut.com

Playmobil
800-351-8697
www.playmobil.com

Playskool
800-752-9755
www.hasbro.com

Tiny Love
888-846-9568
www.tinylove.com

Tonka
800-327-8264
www.hasbro.com

Tyco
800-367-8926
www.mattel.com

Shopping Resources

Here are some of the best Web sites for juvenile products, toys, and apparel.

Juvenile Products

Babies "R" Us
www.babiesrus.com

BabyCenter
www.babycenter.com

More Than One
www.morethan1.com

One Step Ahead
www.onestepahead.com
(catalogue: 800-950-5120)

Perfectly Safe
www.perfectlysafe.com
(catalogue: 800-898-3696)

The Right Start
www.rightstart.com
(catalogue: 800-548-8531)

Safe Beginnings
www.safebeginnings.com
(catalogue: 800-598-8911)

Twins Help!
www.twinshelp.com
(catalogue: 888-448-8842)

Toys and Books

Amazon.com
www.amazon.com

Barnes and Noble
www.bn.com

Borders
www.borders.com

KB Toys
www.kbtoys.com

SmarterKids
www.smarterkids.com

Toys "R" Us
www.toysrus.com

Apparel

babyGap
www.babygap.com

babystyle
www.babystyle.com

biobottoms
www.miabambini.com
(catalogue: 800-766-1254)

Kmart
www.Kmart.com

The Childrens Place
www.childrensplace.com

The Disney Store
www.disneystore.com

Gymboree
www.gymboree.com

Hanna Andersson
www.hannaandersson.com
(catalogue: 800-222-0544)

kidstyle
www.kidstyle.com

Lands' End
www.landsend.com
(catalogue: 800-356-4444)

L.L. Bean
www.llbean.com
(catalogue: 800-552-5437)

Nordstrom
www.nordstrom.com

Old Navy
www.oldnavy.com

Payless ShoeSource
www.payless.com

INDEX

Page numbers in **boldface** refer to illustrations.